Southern Living
OUR BEST
Quick & Easy RECIPES

Southern Living

OUR BEST

Quick & Easy
RECIPES

Compiled by

Jean Wickstrom Liles

Edited by

Lisa Hooper Talley

Oxmoor House®

Library of Congress Catalog Card Number: 96-68834
ISBN: 0-8487-1502-0
Manufactured in the United States of America
First Printing 1996

Editor-in-Chief: Nancy Fitzpatrick Wyatt
Senior Foods Editor: Susan Carlisle Payne
Senior Editor, Editorial Services: Olivia Kindig Wells
Art Director: James Boone

Southern Living Our Best Quick & Easy Recipes

Editor: Lisa Hooper Talley
Copy Editor: Keri Bradford Anderson
Editorial Assistant: Alison Rich Lewis
Director, Test Kitchens: Kathleen Royal Phillips
Assistant Director, Test Kitchens: Gayle Hays Sadler
Test Kitchen Home Economists: Molly Baldwin, Susan Hall Bellows, Julie Christopher,
    Michelle Brown Fuller, Heather Irby, Natalie E. King, Elizabeth Tyler Luckett,
    Jan Moon, Iris Crawley O'Brien, Jan A. Smith
Menu and Recipe Consultant: Jean Wickstrom Liles
Designer: Melissa Jones Clark
Photographer: Jim Bathie
Photo Stylist: Kay E. Clarke
Publishing Systems Administrator: Rick Tucker
Director, Production and Distribution: Phillip Lee
Associate Production Manager: Theresa L. Beste
Production Coordinator: Marianne Jordan Wilson
Production Assistant: Valerie Heard

Cover: *Chicken and Mushrooms Marsala* (page 117)
Back Cover: *Harvest Chowder* (page 140)
Page 2: *Fudge Pie* (page 187)

CONTENTS

Welcome

to *Our Best Quick & Easy Recipes*—a collection of the best timesaving recipes, menus, and tips *Southern Living* has to offer. With this cookbook, you'll get dinner ready and be out of the kitchen faster than ever. All of the recipes feature exact prep and cook times and short ingredient lists grouped to match numbered cooking steps, and most can be on the table in 30 minutes or less. For menus, you'll find menu plans and grocery and equipment lists to make shopping and preparation a snap. And the recipes taste so scrumptious, we're sure this cookbook will be your constant kitchen companion, even when you're not in a hurry.

THE QUICK & EASY KITCHEN

Organization Is the Key

Cut your time preparing meals by organizing your kitchen and by making a game plan that works for you. Start by arranging pantry items, equipment, and utensils for easy access.

Location Is Everything . . .

• **Store** dried herbs and spices in a rack or on a turntable in alphabetical order for speedy identification. Write the purchase date on the container so you'll know when herbs and spices need replacing.

• **Stock** your pantry and refrigerator with staple items. Group similar staples together, rotating older ones to the front to use first. Keep as many labels as possible in view for at-a-glace inventory.

• **Attach** a magnetic shopping list to the refrigerator door for jotting down items you need to purchase.

• **Keep** a cutting board on the counter near the sink, ready for use at a moment's notice.

• **Store** wooden spoons, plastic scrapers, rubber and metal spatulas, tongs, wire whisks, cooking spoons and forks, kitchen shears, a basting brush, and a ladle in large decorative crocks or jars near your cooktop and mixing center.

• **Place** aluminum foil, plastic wrap, wax paper, and food storage bags in a drawer or in a rack inside a cabinet door near your main work area.

• **Save** counter space by using stackable canisters for flour, sugar, and coffee. Keep a set of measuring cups and spoons in the flour and sugar containers.

• **Hang** pot holders next to the oven, cooktop, and microwave oven for quick grabbing. Keep a trivet on the counter near the oven for hot foods.

• **Stand** baking sheets and pans, cakepans and piepans, muffin pans, and cooling racks in a wire dish drainer in an under-the-counter cabinet.

Neatness Counts . . .

• **Organize** your recipe files. Try those recipes you've been saving, and discard those you know you'll never use. Make a separate file for quick and easy recipes.

• **Measure** ingredients onto wax paper or paper plates for easy cleanup.

• **Mount** a paper towel holder, a coffeemaker, and other compact kitchen appliances under the cabinet to save space and to eliminate counter clutter.

• **Use** plastic drawer dividers to separate small utensils from large ones.

• **Keep** knives sharpened and stored in a safe, convenient holder on the countertop or in a drawer.

• **Save** cleanup time and avoid a huge stack of dishes in the sink later by cleaning up as you cook.

Freeze Spicy Vegetable-Beef Soup (page 138) to enjoy later.

COOK NOW—SERVE LATER

The *Southern Living* Test Kitchens staff prepares hundreds of recipes each week. And over the years, we've discovered time-savers that streamline meal preparation both at work *and* at home. Here are a few of our favorite secrets:

• **Freeze** single servings of soup, stew, chili, and spaghetti sauce in microwave-safe containers.

• **Bake** a double batch of muffins, waffles, or pancakes, and freeze the leftovers up to one month. Reheat in the toaster oven or microwave oven.

• **Cook** extra rice, and freeze in individual or family-size portions up to one month. Simply microwave to thaw.

• **Chop** extra green pepper and onion to freeze. Spread a thin layer of the vegetables on a baking sheet; freeze the vegetables 30 minutes or until frozen solid. Crumble them into zip-top freezer bags; freeze up to three months. Scoop out to measure.

• **Process** extra breadcrumbs or chopped nuts while you have the food processor out, and store in the freezer.

• **Keep** a container of cut-up brownies in the freezer. For an instant dessert, pop a brownie into the microwave; top with vanilla ice cream and hot fudge sauce.

• **Cook** the rest of a package of bacon while you prepare some for breakfast. Layer the cooled slices between sheets of wax paper in an airtight container, and freeze. Reheat the slices in the microwave.

• **Keep** browned ground chuck on hand in the freezer. Drain the browned meat, and spread in a thin layer on a baking sheet. Freeze 45 minutes. Crumble the meat into a zip-top freezer bag, label, and freeze up to three months. You can then quickly prepare chili, spaghetti, and casseroles.

TAKE STOCK Keep basic ingredients and equipment on hand for a well-stocked kitchen.

Baking Supplies
- baking powder and baking soda
- biscuit and baking mix
- bread mixes
- chocolate: cocoa, semisweet morsels and squares, unsweetened squares
- coconut: flaked
- cornmeal
- cornstarch
- syrups: corn, maple
- evaporated milk
- extracts: almond, vanilla
- flour: all-purpose, cake, self-rising
- honey
- sugar: brown, granulated, powdered
- yeast

Condiments
- chili sauce
- horseradish
- hot sauce
- jams, jellies, preserves
- ketchup
- marinades
- mayonnaise, salad dressings
- mustards: Dijon, prepared
- salsa
- soy sauce
- vinegars: cider, red wine, white
- Worcestershire sauce

Cooking Supplies
- bouillon cubes or granules
- breadcrumbs: dry
- broths, canned: beef, chicken
- garlic: bottled, fresh
- herbs: bay leaves; chili, curry, and garlic powder; dried basil, Italian seasoning, oregano, parsley flakes, rosemary, tarragon, and thyme; garlic salt; ground cumin; dry mustard; paprika
- nuts: assorted
- oils: olive, vegetable
- peanut butter
- pepper: ground black, red, and white; black peppercorns
- salt and seasoned salt

- shortening
- soup: cream of mushroom
- soup mix: onion
- spaghetti sauce
- spices: ground allspice, cinnamon, cloves, ginger, and nutmeg
- tea bags and coffee
- tomato paste and sauce
- vegetable cooking spray

Dairy Products
- butter and margarine
- cheeses: Cheddar, cream, mozzarella, Parmesan, Swiss
- eggs
- milk
- sour cream
- whipping cream
- yogurt: plain

Fruits and Vegetables
- beans and peas: dried, frozen
- fruits: canned, dried, fresh
- green pepper: frozen chopped
- lemon juice: bottled fresh
- mushrooms: canned
- onions: fresh, frozen chopped
- orange juice concentrate: frozen
- potatoes: fresh
- salad fixings
- tomatoes: canned whole
- vegetables: assorted, frozen

Grains and Pastas
- breads: frozen, refrigerated
- grains: couscous, grits, oats, rice
- pastas: egg noodles, fettuccine, penne, spaghetti
- rice and pasta side-dish mixes

Meats and Poultry
- bacon
- canned chicken
- canned tuna
- ground chuck
- shrimp: frozen, peeled and deveined
- skinned and boned chicken breast halves

Bakeware and Cookware
- baking pans and dishes: 8- and 9-inch round and square, 11- x 7- x 1½-inch, 13- x 9- x 2-inch
- casseroles: 1- to 3-quart
- cookie sheets, jelly roll pan
- custard cups
- double boiler
- Dutch oven with lid, stock pot
- loaf pans: 8½- x 4½- x 3-inch, 9- x 5- x 3-inch
- muffin tins
- pieplate: 9-inch
- roasting pan with rack
- saucepans with lids: 1-quart (small), 2-quart (medium), 3-quart (large)
- skillets: 8-inch (small), 10-inch (medium), 12-inch (large)
- springform pan: 9-inch
- tube pan or Bundt pan

Other Equipment
- basting brush
- colander and strainer
- cutters: biscuit, cookie
- cutting board
- garlic press
- grater
- juicer
- kitchen shears
- knives: carving, chef's (6- to 8-inch), paring, serrated bread
- ladle
- measuring cups: dry, liquid
- mixing and measuring spoons
- mixing bowl set
- openers: bottle, can, corkscrew
- pastry blender
- rolling pin
- sifter
- spatulas: metal, rubber
- steamer basket
- thermometers: candy/deep-fry, meat
- timer
- tongs
- vegetable peeler
- wire racks
- wire whisk

SHORTCUT STRATEGIES

You don't have to spend hours in the kitchen. Here are our favorite ways to streamline meal preparation:

Streamline with Techniques . . .

• **Read** the recipe, and assemble all the ingredients and equipment before starting.
• **Measure** dry ingredients before wet ones to minimize cleanup.
• **Rinse** the measuring cup or spoon with hot water before measuring honey; the honey will then slide right out.
• **Buy** packages of sliced meat at the meat counter for stir-frying.
• **Shape** patties for burgers in a flash (below). Shape ground beef into a log, freeze partially, and slice. Wrap individually, or stack with layers of wax paper between burgers in an airtight container; freeze up to three months.

Processing double amounts of ingredients

Shaping patties for burgers

• **Chop** an ingredient used in two recipes within a menu only once (above). For example, if you'll need ½ cup chopped onion for two recipes, go ahead and chop 1 cup.
• **Chop** or grind dry ingredients like breadcrumbs or nuts in a food processor first; you can then chop or shred moist foods without having to wash the workbowl.
• **Purchase** ingredients in their closest-to-usable form, such as skinned and boned chicken breast halves, peeled shrimp, and shredded cheese. Buy cut vegetables in the produce department or at the salad bar.
• **Slice** vegetables like carrots, green onions, or celery three or four pieces at a time.
• **Peel** a tomato or peach by dipping the fruit into boiling water for 15 to 30 seconds; the skin will slip off easily.
• **Substitute** ready-to-serve chicken and beef broth for homemade stock.
• **Use** refrigerated or fresh pasta; it cooks faster than dried. Boil-in-bag rice cooks in half the time of regular rice.

Streamline with Equipment . . .

• **Keep** two sets of both dry and liquid measuring cups and spoons on hand so you can measure consecutive ingredients without repeatedly washing or wiping out the measure.

• **Use** a salad spinner to spin-dry lettuce and other vegetables.

• **Keep** a swivel-bladed vegetable peeler handy for tasks other than peeling vegetables. Use it to shred a small amount of cheese, remove strings from celery stalks, or make quick chocolate curls.

• **Make** cracker crumbs or cookie crumbs quickly without a food processor. Place crackers or cookies in a heavy-duty, zip-top plastic bag; seal bag, and roll with a rolling pin or pound gently with a meat mallet.

• **Use** a pastry blender to mash avocados for chunky guacamole (below) or to slice butter and hard-cooked eggs.

Mashing avocados with a pastry blender

Chopping tomatoes in the can

• **Chop** tomatoes right in the can with kitchen shears (above).

• **Tenderize** and flatten meat quickly with a meat mallet.

• **Place** a metal colander upside down over the skillet when frying; this will prevent splatters while allowing steam to escape.

• **Use** a food processor to chop, slice, or shred several ingredients consecutively without washing the workbowl if the ingredients will later be combined.

• **Cut** day-old bread into cubes for croutons using a pizza cutter—it's faster than using a knife.

• **Preheat** the oven when baking or roasting to save time. The oven can reach the specified temperature while you're preparing the recipe.

• **Use** nonstick cookware and bakeware for easy cleanup.

• **Thaw** frozen foods, soften butter, melt chocolate, and heat liquids quickly in a microwave oven.

"Herb Garden Dinner" menu
(page 37)

Quick
MENUS

Does the thought of entertaining during the week make you stressed? Would you like to have a few friends over this weekend without spending your entire Saturday in the kitchen? You can relax with these incredibly wonderful,

COMPANY'S COMING

but quick, menus; they'll take you from brunch to lunch to dinner without a lot of fuss. All six menus can be on the table—start to finish—in one hour or less. And each menu has a grocery list, equipment list, and foolproof menu plan to make it easier for you.

"Sunset Supper" menu features Chicken Provolone, Endive-Tomato Starburst Salad, and Rice and Asparagus. (Menu begins on page 33.)

MEXICAN BRUNCH

Mexicana Brunch Pie

Fresh Fruit   Marmalade Coffee Cake

Mexican Coffee

Serves 6

GROCERIES NEEDED

Check staples: all-purpose flour, brown sugar (light and dark), baking powder, ground cinnamon, ground nutmeg, vanilla extract, milk, eggs, butter or margarine

- Assorted fresh fruit
- 1 (4.5-ounce) can chopped green chiles
- ¾ cup orange marmalade
- ½ cup ground dark roast coffee
- ⅓ cup chocolate syrup
- 2 tablespoons chopped walnuts
- 1 (12-ounce) carton small-curd cottage cheese
- 2 cups (8 ounces) shredded Monterey Jack cheese
- 2 (10-ounce) cans refrigerated buttermilk biscuits
- Frozen whipped topping

EQUIPMENT NEEDED

- Electric mixer
- 9-inch pieplate
- 12-cup Bundt pan
- Electric coffeemaker
- Large saucepan

Brunch is a wonderful way to entertain because it can be as formal or as casual as you choose. Make this leisurely south-of-the-border menu the highlight of a fun weekend spent with friends and family.

MENU PLAN

1 Prepare Mexicana Brunch Pie.

2 While pie bakes for 10 minutes at 400°, prepare Marmalade Coffee Cake. Reduce oven temperature to 350°. Continue baking pie, and place coffee cake in oven on same rack with pie.

3 Complete step 1 of Mexican Coffee.

4 Arrange fresh fruit on a serving tray.

5 Complete step 2 of Mexican Coffee.

From front: Mexicana Brunch Pie with fresh fruit, Mexican Coffee, Marmalade Coffee Cake (Recipes begin on following page.)

Mexicana Brunch Pie

PREP: **9** MINUTES; BAKE: **35** MINUTES

¼ cup all-purpose flour
½ teaspoon baking powder
2 tablespoons butter or
    margarine, melted
5 large eggs

1 (12-ounce) carton small-curd
    cottage cheese
1 (4.5-ounce) can chopped green
    chiles, undrained
2 cups (8 ounces) shredded
    Monterey Jack cheese

1 Combine first 4 ingredients in a large mixing bowl; beat at medium speed of an electric mixer until well blended.

2 Stir in cottage cheese, chiles, and Monterey Jack cheese; pour into a well-greased 9-inch pieplate.

3 Bake at 400° for 10 minutes. Reduce oven temperature to 350°; bake 25 to 27 minutes or until set. Yield: 6 servings.

Marmalade Coffee Cake

PREP: **16** MINUTES; BAKE: **33** MINUTES

FYI

The marmalade will stick to the Bundt pan if the pan isn't well greased. A heavy coating of vegetable cooking spray should do the trick; just be sure the spray gets into every crevice of the pan.

¾ cup orange marmalade
2 tablespoons chopped walnuts

¾ cup firmly packed light brown
    sugar
¾ teaspoon ground cinnamon
2 (10-ounce) cans refrigerated
    buttermilk biscuits
½ cup butter or margarine,
    melted

1 Spread marmalade in bottom of a greased 12-cup Bundt pan; sprinkle with walnuts.

2 Combine brown sugar and cinnamon in a small bowl. Separate biscuits; dip in melted butter, and dredge in brown sugar mixture. Stand biscuits on edge around pan, flat sides out, spacing evenly. Fill in with remaining biscuits. Drizzle remaining butter over biscuits, and sprinkle with remaining brown sugar mixture.

3 Bake at 350° for 33 to 35 minutes or until golden. Cool in pan on a wire rack 5 minutes. Invert onto a serving platter, and serve immediately. Yield: one 10-inch coffee cake.

Mexican Coffee

PREP: 12 MINUTES; COOK: 5 MINUTES

½ cup ground dark roast coffee
1 tablespoon ground cinnamon
¼ teaspoon ground nutmeg
5 cups water

1 cup milk
⅓ cup chocolate syrup
¼ cup firmly packed dark brown
    sugar
1 teaspoon vanilla extract
Frozen whipped topping, thawed
Additional ground cinnamon

1 Place coffee in filter basket of coffeemaker; add 1 tablespoon ground cinnamon and nutmeg. Add water to coffeemaker; brew coffee according to manufacturer's instructions.

2 Combine milk, chocolate syrup, and sugar in a large saucepan; cook over low heat, stirring constantly, until sugar dissolves. Stir in brewed coffee and vanilla. Pour immediately into mugs, and top each serving with a dollop of whipped topping. Sprinkle with additional ground cinnamon. Yield: 6 cups.

Mexican Coffee

CELEBRATION LUNCHEON

Spinach Salad

Chicken with Champagne Sauce

Lemon Vegetables   Rolls

Fresh Fruit with Brandied Chocolate Sauce

Serves 6

GROCERIES NEEDED

Check staples: salt, black pepper, ground white pepper, ground cinnamon, butter or margarine

Optional garnish: fresh tarragon sprigs

- 4 small new potatoes
- 2 carrots
- 2 yellow squash
- 1 zucchini
- 1 cup sliced fresh mushrooms
- 1 tablespoon grated lemon rind
- 3 tablespoons lemon juice
- Makings for a spinach salad
- Assorted fresh fruits
- 1 (12-ounce) package semisweet chocolate morsels
- 1 tablespoon instant coffee granules
- Commercial rolls
- 6 skinned and boned chicken breast halves
- ½ cup sour cream
- ½ cup whipping cream
- ½ cup champagne
- ¼ cup brandy

EQUIPMENT NEEDED

- Large skillet with lid
- Small saucepan
- Steamer basket

Simply elegant, yet elegantly simple, this luncheon menu is an effortless way to celebrate an important event.

MENU PLAN

1 Cut up fruits for dessert, and prepare spinach salad; cover and chill.

2 Complete steps 1 and 2 of Chicken with Champagne Sauce.

3 While chicken simmers, cut up and steam vegetables for Lemon Vegetables.

4 Prepare Brandied Chocolate Sauce; keep warm.

5 Heat rolls.

6 Complete step 3 of Chicken with Champagne Sauce.

7 Complete step 2 of Lemon Vegetables.

Chicken with Champagne Sauce, Lemon Vegetables, rolls (Recipes begin on following page.)

Chicken with Champagne Sauce

PREP: 3 MINUTES; COOK: 30 MINUTES

6 skinned and boned chicken
    breast halves
3 tablespoons butter or
    margarine, melted
1 cup sliced fresh mushrooms
½ cup champagne

½ cup sour cream
¼ teaspoon salt
¼ teaspoon ground white pepper
Garnish: fresh tarragon sprigs

1 Cook chicken in butter in a large skillet over medium-high heat until browned on both sides. Remove chicken, reserving drippings in skillet. Add mushrooms to drippings; cook, stirring constantly, until tender. Stir in champagne.

2 Return chicken to skillet. Bring mixture to a boil; cover, reduce heat, and simmer 20 minutes or until chicken is done.

3 Transfer chicken to a serving platter, reserving mushroom mixture in skillet. Add sour cream, salt, and pepper to mushroom mixture. Bring to a boil; reduce heat, and simmer, stirring constantly, 5 minutes or until mixture is thickened. Spoon mushroom mixture over chicken. Garnish, if desired. Yield: 6 servings.

Lemon Vegetables

PREP: 10 MINUTES; COOK: 10 MINUTES

4 small new potatoes, unpeeled
    and sliced
2 carrots, scraped and cut into
    thin strips
2 yellow squash, cut into thin
    strips
1 zucchini, sliced crosswise

⅓ cup butter or margarine,
    melted
1 tablespoon grated lemon rind
3 tablespoons lemon juice
¼ teaspoon salt
⅛ teaspoon pepper

1 Arrange potato and carrot in a steamer basket over boiling water; cover and steam 8 minutes. Add yellow squash and zucchini; cover and steam 2 minutes or until vegetables are crisp-tender. Place vegetables in a serving bowl.

2 Combine butter and remaining 4 ingredients; pour over vegetables, and toss gently. Serve immediately. Yield: 6 servings.

FYI

Slice carrots, yellow squash, and zucchini beforehand, and chill in zip-top plastic bags. Or buy cut and sliced vegetables to save even more time.

Brandied Chocolate Sauce

PREP: 1 MINUTE; COOK: 9 MINUTES

½ cup whipping cream
¼ cup brandy
2 tablespoons water
1 (12-ounce) package semisweet
    chocolate morsels

1 tablespoon instant coffee
    granules
Dash of ground cinnamon

1 Combine first 4 ingredients in a small saucepan; cook over low heat until chocolate melts and mixture is smooth, stirring often.

2 Add coffee granules and cinnamon to chocolate mixture, stirring until well blended. Serve warm with fresh fruit. Yield: 1¾ cups.

DINNER ON THE DECK

Grilled Flank Steak

Salt-Roasted New Potatoes

Lemon Carrot Sticks   Dinner Rolls

Strawberry Delight

Serves 6

GROCERIES NEEDED

Check staples: sugar, brown sugar, vegetable oil, salt, butter or margarine

Optional garnish: lemon zest

- 1½ pounds carrots
- 18 new potatoes
- 1½ cups sliced fresh strawberries
- 1 tablespoon minced garlic
- 1 tablespoon minced fresh ginger
- ⅓ cup lemon juice
- ½ cup soy sauce
- 1 tablespoon kosher salt

- 1 (1½-pound) flank steak
- 1 quart pineapple sherbet
- Dinner rolls
- ¾ cup champagne or sparkling white grape juice
- ¼ cup dry red wine

EQUIPMENT NEEDED

- Grill with lid
- 15- x 10- x 1-inch jellyroll pan

- Basting brush
- Steamer basket
- Small saucepan

Capture the flavor of summer by grilling outdoors. You'll spend more time out on the deck with your guests—and less time in the kitchen.

MENU PLAN

1 Complete steps 1 and 2 of Grilled Flank Steak.

2 Prepare Salt-Roasted New Potatoes.

3 While potatoes roast, prepare Lemon Carrot Sticks.

4 While potatoes roast and carrots cook, grill flank steak; let stand 5 minutes before slicing.

5 While steak grills, heat rolls.

6 Prepare Strawberry Delight just before serving.

Grilled Flank Steak, Lemon Carrot Sticks, Salt-Roasted New Potatoes
(Recipes begin on following page.)

Grilled Flank Steak

PREP: 12 MINUTES; MARINATE: 8 HOURS; GRILL: 10 MINUTES

FYI

If you don't keep wine on hand, buy wine splits (6.4 ounces or one-fourth of a standard wine bottle) for this marinade. You'll find splits easier to store — and quicker to use up.

1 (1½-pound) flank steak

½ cup firmly packed brown sugar
½ cup vegetable oil
½ cup soy sauce
¼ cup dry red wine
1 tablespoon minced garlic
1 tablespoon minced fresh
   ginger

1 Make shallow cuts in steak diagonally across grain at 1-inch intervals. Place steak in a shallow dish or heavy-duty, zip-top plastic bag.

2 Combine brown sugar and remaining 5 ingredients; pour over steak. Cover dish, or seal bag. Marinate in refrigerator 8 hours, turning meat occasionally.

3 Remove steak from marinade, reserving marinade. Place marinade in a small saucepan; bring to a boil, and remove from heat. Grill steak, covered, over medium-hot coals (350° to 400°) 5 minutes on each side or to desired degree of doneness, basting twice with marinade. Let stand 5 minutes before slicing diagonally across grain into thin slices. Yield: 6 servings.

Salt-Roasted New Potatoes

PREP: 5 MINUTES; BAKE: 25 MINUTES

FYI

To preserve vitamins and to save time, leave the skins on the potatoes.

18 new potatoes, unpeeled and
   halved
1 tablespoon vegetable oil
1 tablespoon kosher salt

1 Place potato halves, cut sides down, in a lightly greased 15- x 10- x 1-inch jellyroll pan. Brush potatoes with oil, and sprinkle with salt. Bake at 450° for 25 minutes or until tender, turning after 15 minutes. Yield: 6 servings.

Lemon Carrot Sticks

PREP: 22 MINUTES; COOK: 8 MINUTES

1½ pounds carrots, scraped and
    cut into 3-inch sticks

⅓ cup lemon juice
3 tablespoons butter or
    margarine, melted
2 tablespoons sugar
¼ teaspoon salt
Garnish: lemon zest

1 Arrange carrot sticks in a steamer basket over boiling water. Cover and steam 8 minutes or until crisp-tender.

2 While carrot cooks, combine lemon juice, butter, sugar, and salt in a small saucepan; bring to a boil. Reduce heat, and simmer, uncovered, 1 minute. Transfer carrot to a serving bowl. Pour lemon juice mixture over carrot sticks, and toss gently. Garnish, if desired. Serve immediately. Yield: 6 servings.

F/I

Cut the carrots into 3-inch sticks ahead of time. Place the carrot sticks in a zip-top plastic bag, and chill.

Strawberry Delight

PREP: 11 MINUTES

1 quart pineapple sherbet
1½ cups sliced fresh
    strawberries
¾ cup champagne or sparkling
    white grape juice

1 Spoon sherbet evenly into 6 stemmed glasses. Top each serving with ¼ cup strawberries. Pour champagne over each serving. Serve immediately. Yield: 6 servings.

FESTIVE SPRING DINNER

Shish Kabobs

Tabbouleh Salad   *Hummus with Pita Wedges*

Baklava

Serves 4

GROCERIES NEEDED

Check staples: olive oil, salt, pepper, hot sauce

Optional garnish: fresh mint sprigs

- 12 fresh Sugar Snap peas
- 3 green onions
- 3 cloves garlic
- 2 medium tomatoes
- 1 purple onion
- ¼ pound fresh mushrooms
- 1¼ cups chopped fresh parsley
- ¾ cup chopped onion
- ½ cup chopped fresh mint

- 2 (15-ounce) cans garbanzo beans
- ½ (15¼-ounce) can spear pineapple
- About 1 cup lemon juice
- 1 cup bulgur wheat
- 1 pound boneless leg of lamb
- Pita wedges
- Commercial baklava

EQUIPMENT NEEDED

- 4 (15-inch) metal skewers
- Grill with lid
- Basting brush
- Food processor

Celebrate spring with this menu. You can prepare most of the recipes in advance; all you'll need to do to serve them is one or two last-minute steps. Stop by the bakery on the way home from work, and pick up baklava for dessert.

MENU PLAN

1 Complete steps 1 and 2 of Tabbouleh Salad.

2 Prepare Hummus; chill until serving time. Toast pita wedges.

3 Prepare Shish Kabobs.

4 Just before serving, complete step 3 of Tabbouleh Salad.

Shish Kabobs, Tabbouleh Salad, Hummus with Pita Wedges
(Recipes begin on following page.)

Shish Kabobs

PREP: 20 MINUTES; MARINATE: 3 HOURS; GRILL: 5 MINUTES

Marinate the lamb in a heavy-duty, zip-top plastic bag to cut cleanup time.

1 pound boneless leg of lamb, cut into 1-inch cubes
⅓ cup lemon juice
¼ cup finely chopped onion
¼ cup olive oil
1 teaspoon salt

1 purple onion, cut into 8 wedges
12 fresh Sugar Snap peas
¼ pound fresh mushrooms
½ (15¼-ounce) can spear pineapple, drained and cut in half

1 Place lamb in a large heavy-duty, zip-top plastic bag. Combine lemon juice and next 3 ingredients. Pour half of lemon juice mixture over lamb; chill remaining half of mixture. Seal bag; marinate in refrigerator 3 hours, turning bag occasionally.

2 Remove lamb from marinade; discard marinade. Alternately thread lamb, onion wedges, peas, mushrooms, and pineapple onto 4 (15-inch) metal skewers. Grill kabobs, covered, over medium coals (300° to 350°) 5 to 10 minutes or to desired degree of doneness, turning and basting with chilled lemon juice mixture. Yield: 4 servings.

Tabbouleh Salad

PREP: 30 MINUTES; CHILL: 8 HOURS

2 cups hot water
1 cup bulgur wheat, uncooked

1 cup chopped fresh parsley
½ cup chopped fresh mint
½ cup chopped onion
⅓ cup lemon juice
2 tablespoons olive oil
½ teaspoon salt
½ teaspoon pepper

2 medium tomatoes, finely chopped
Garnish: fresh mint sprigs

1 Pour hot water over bulgur; let stand 30 minutes. Drain well.

2 Combine bulgur, parsley, and next 6 ingredients in a large bowl; cover and chill at least 8 hours.

3 Just before serving, stir in tomato. Garnish, if desired. Yield: 6 cups.

Hummus with Pita Wedges

PREP: 10 MINUTES; CHILL: 3 HOURS

3 green onions, sliced
3 cloves garlic

2 (15-ounce) cans garbanzo beans, drained
¼ cup chopped fresh parsley
2 tablespoons lemon juice
½ teaspoon salt
½ teaspoon pepper
Dash of hot sauce

¼ cup olive oil

1 Position knife blade in food processor bowl; add green onions and garlic. Process until onions are minced.

2 Add beans and next 5 ingredients to onion mixture; process until smooth, stopping once to scrape down sides.

3 Pour oil through food chute with processor running, blending just until mixture is smooth. Spoon hummus into a large serving bowl; cover and chill at least 3 hours. Serve with toasted pita wedges. Yield: 2½ cups.

Use your food processor to prepare this recipe quickly.

Tabbouleh Salad (facing page)

SUNSET SUPPER

Chicken Provolone

Rice and Asparagus

Endive-Tomato Starburst Salad

Merlot Ice

Serves 6

GROCERIES NEEDED

Check staples: sugar, olive oil, salt, pepper

Optional garnish: fresh rosemary sprigs

- 8 plum tomatoes
- 6 heads Belgian endive
- 1 medium onion
- 1 sprig fresh rosemary
- 1½ pounds fresh asparagus
- 2 tablespoons stone-ground mustard
- ¼ cup red wine vinegar
- ¼ cup sherry vinegar
- 1 cup long-grain rice
- 3½ cups chicken broth
- 6 skinned and boned chicken breast halves
- 6 slices prosciutto
- 6 ounces provolone cheese
- 1½ cups Merlot

EQUIPMENT NEEDED

- Grill with lid
- Medium saucepan with lid
- Large skillet
- Jar with lid
- 8-inch square pan
- Food processor

Gracious entertaining is easy with this summertime menu. Invite guests to mingle outdoors and to sip glasses of white wine while the chicken grills and while you put the final quick touches on the side dishes.

MENU PLAN

1 Prepare Merlot Ice, and complete step 1 of Endive-Tomato Starburst Salad the day before.

2 Complete steps 2 and 3 of Endive-Tomato Starburst Salad; cover and chill until serving time.

3 Complete step 1 of Rice and Asparagus; keep warm.

4 Prepare Chicken Provolone.

5 While chicken grills, complete steps 2 and 3 of Rice and Asparagus.

6 Complete step 4 of Endive-Tomato Starburst Salad.

Endive-Tomato Starburst Salad (page 35)

Chicken Provolone

PREP: 5 MINUTES; GRILL: 20 MINUTES

6 skinned and boned chicken
    breast halves

6 slices prosciutto
6 ounces provolone cheese,
    shredded
Garnish: fresh rosemary sprigs

1 Grill chicken, uncovered, over medium-hot coals (350° to 400°) 15 minutes, turning once.

2 Top each breast with a prosciutto slice; sprinkle evenly with cheese. Cover and grill 5 minutes or until cheese melts. Garnish, if desired. Yield: 6 servings.

Rice and Asparagus

PREP: 10 MINUTES; COOK: 20 MINUTES

1 medium onion, chopped
2 tablespoons olive oil
3½ cups chicken broth, divided
½ teaspoon salt
¼ teaspoon pepper
1 cup long-grain rice, uncooked
1 sprig fresh rosemary

1½ pounds fresh asparagus

1 Cook onion in hot oil in a medium saucepan over medium-high heat, stirring constantly, 3 minutes or until tender. Add 2 cups broth, salt, and pepper; bring to a boil. Stir in rice and rosemary. Cover, reduce heat, and simmer 20 to 25 minutes or until rice is tender and liquid is absorbed.

2 Snap off tough ends of asparagus. Remove scales from stalks with a knife or vegetable peeler, if desired. Cut asparagus diagonally into 1-inch pieces. Combine asparagus and remaining 1½ cups chicken broth in a large skillet; cook, uncovered, over medium-high heat 6 to 8 minutes or until crisp-tender. Drain.

3 Remove rosemary sprig from rice mixture; discard. Combine rice mixture and asparagus; toss gently. Serve immediately. Yield: 6 servings.

Endive-Tomato Starburst Salad

PREP: 15 MINUTES

½ cup olive oil
¼ cup red wine vinegar
¼ cup sherry vinegar
2 tablespoons stone-ground
    mustard
⅛ teaspoon pepper

6 heads Belgian endive

8 plum tomatoes

1 Combine first 5 ingredients in a jar; cover tightly, and shake vigorously. Chill, if desired.

2 Remove 4 outer leaves from each head of endive; arrange leaves in a starburst pattern on a serving platter. Thinly slice remaining endive; set sliced endive aside.

3 Thinly slice tomatoes lengthwise; arrange tomato slices on endive leaves. Place sliced endive in center of platter.

4 Drizzle salad with dressing mixture. Yield: 6 servings.

Prepare the dressing mixture in advance to allow the flavors to blend.

Merlot Ice

PREP: 10 MINUTES; FREEZE: 6 HOURS

3 cups water
¾ cup sugar
1½ cups Merlot

1 Combine water and sugar in a medium saucepan; bring to a boil, stirring occasionally. Remove from heat; let cool. Stir in wine. Pour mixture into an 8-inch square pan. Cover and freeze 3 hours or until firm, stirring occasionally.

2 Break frozen mixture into chunks. Position knife blade in food processor bowl; add chunks, and process until smooth, stopping once to scrape down sides. Return slush mixture to pan; cover and freeze 3 hours or until firm. To serve, spoon ice into individual dessert dishes. Yield: 4 cups.

Pinched for time? Make Merlot Ice up to a month ahead, and freeze. Or purchase commercial lemon sorbet as a substitute. Dress up your dessert by serving it in a compote and by garnishing it with a mint sprig.

HERB GARDEN DINNER

Peppered Goat Cheese

Grilled Herbed Salmon Steaks

Tomato-Basil Pasta   French Bread

Amaretto Crème with Fresh Fruit

Serves 8

GROCERIES NEEDED

Check staples: all-purpose flour, sugar, olive oil, salt, freshly ground pepper, cracked pepper, vanilla extract, milk, butter or margarine, eggs

Optional garnishes: fresh basil, oregano, and mint

- 4 cloves garlic
- 3 tomatoes
- ½ cup chopped fresh basil
- 2 teaspoons chopped fresh thyme
- 2 teaspoons chopped fresh marjoram
- 2 teaspoons chopped fresh sage
- 2 teaspoons chopped fresh parsley
- Fresh peaches
- Fresh raspberries
- 1 (16-ounce) package linguine
- ½ cup plus 2 teaspoons lemon juice
- French baguette loaf
- French bread
- 8 (6-ounce) salmon steaks (1 inch thick)
- 1 (10-ounce) package goat cheese
- 1 cup dry white wine
- 1 tablespoon amaretto

EQUIPMENT NEEDED

- Jar with lid
- Grill with lid
- Basting brush
- Large saucepan
- Colander
- Medium saucepan

If you grow fresh herbs, you can put your garden in the spotlight with this warm-weather dinner. Snip an abundance of fresh herbs to use in these recipes; then savor the wonderful aromas and flavors they'll add to your menu.

MENU PLAN

1 Make Amaretto Crème; chill.

2 Prepare Peppered Goat Cheese; set aside.

3 Prepare Grilled Herbed Salmon Steaks; keep warm.

4 While salmon grills, prepare Tomato-Basil Pasta. Heat bread, if desired.

5 Just before serving, prepare fruit for dessert.

Grilled Herbed Salmon Steaks, Tomato-Basil Pasta, French bread (Recipes begin on following page.)

Peppered Goat Cheese

PREP: 5 MINUTES

1 (10-ounce) package goat cheese
1 to 2 teaspoons cracked pepper

Garnish: fresh oregano sprigs

1 Roll goat cheese in pepper to coat.

2 Place cheese on a small serving plate; garnish, if desired. Serve cheese with French baguette slices. Yield: 8 appetizer servings.

Grilled Herbed Salmon Steaks

PREP: 7 MINUTES; GRILL: 14 MINUTES

⅓ cup dry white wine
⅓ cup olive oil
2 teaspoons chopped fresh thyme
2 teaspoons chopped fresh
    marjoram
2 teaspoons chopped fresh sage
2 teaspoons chopped fresh
    parsley
2 teaspoons lemon juice
½ teaspoon salt
⅛ teaspoon freshly ground
    pepper

8 (6-ounce) salmon steaks
    (1 inch thick)
Garnish: fresh basil sprigs

1 Combine first 9 ingredients in a small jar; cover tightly, and shake vigorously.

2 Grill fish, covered, over medium-hot coals (350° to 400°) 7 to 8 minutes on each side or until fish flakes easily when tested with a fork, basting with herb mixture. Garnish, if desired. Yield: 8 servings.

Note: Substitute ¾ teaspoon each of dried thyme, marjoram, rubbed sage, and parsley flakes for the fresh herbs listed at left, if desired.

Tomato-Basil Pasta

PREP: 10 MINUTES; COOK: 10 MINUTES

1 (16-ounce) package linguine, uncooked

2 tablespoons butter or margarine
4 cloves garlic, minced
2 cups seeded, finely chopped tomato
½ cup chopped fresh basil
½ cup dry white wine
½ cup lemon juice

1 Cook pasta according to package directions; drain.

2 While pasta cooks, melt butter in a large saucepan over medium heat; add garlic, and cook, stirring constantly, 1 minute. Remove from heat; stir in tomato and remaining 3 ingredients. Toss pasta with tomato mixture. Yield: 8 servings.

Cook the linguine a day ahead; drain and toss with 1 tablespoon olive oil. Cover and chill. To reheat, microwave, covered, at HIGH about 2 minutes.

Amaretto Crème with Fresh Fruit

PREP: 25 MINUTES; COOK: 10 MINUTES; CHILL: 10 MINUTES

4 egg yolks, lightly beaten
½ cup sugar
2 tablespoons all-purpose flour
1 cup milk

1 tablespoon amaretto
½ teaspoon vanilla extract
Sliced fresh peaches
Fresh raspberries
Garnish: fresh mint sprigs

1 Combine first 3 ingredients in a medium saucepan; gradually add milk, stirring until smooth. Cook mixture over medium heat, stirring constantly, 10 minutes or until thickened and bubbly.

2 Remove from heat, and stir in amaretto and vanilla. Place pan in a bowl of ice. Chill about 10 minutes, stirring often. Serve with peach slices and raspberries or your choice of fresh fruit. Garnish, if desired. Yield: 1½ cups.

To peel peaches quickly, dip them into boiling water for 30 seconds; the skins will slip off easily when you use a paring knife.

If you're looking for streamlined suppers that are ready in a flash, your search ends here. These everyday menus are designed for speed—but they don't skimp on flavor. Sometimes the best meals require few ingredients and

WHAT'S FOR SUPPER?

little prep time. Our supper menus contain two or three recipes and a commercial side dish or dessert suggestion. The best part? Supper's on the table in 45 minutes or less.

"Festive Family Supper" menu features Steak Parmesan, steamed broccoli, Cream Cheese and Onion Mashed Potatoes. (Menu begins on page 47.)

SEAFARE SPECIAL

Mahimahi in Grape Sauce

Asparagus-Tomato Salad   Rolls

Amaretto Breeze

Serves 4

GROCERIES NEEDED

Check staples: all-purpose flour, salt, pepper, butter or margarine

- 1 pound fresh asparagus
- 12 cherry tomatoes
- 8 romaine lettuce leaves
- 1½ cups seedless green grapes
- ⅓ cup commercial reduced-calorie Italian salad dressing
- Rice
- Bakery rolls
- 4 (½-pound) mahimahi fillets
- ¼ cup freshly grated Parmesan cheese
- 1½ quarts vanilla ice cream
- ½ cup dry vermouth
- ⅓ cup amaretto
- ⅓ cup brandy

EQUIPMENT NEEDED

- Large skillet with lid
- Steamer basket
- Electric blender

When you've got to have dinner in a hurry for last-minute guests, remember this menu. You'll be able to relax and enjoy your company with a meal that centers on delicately flavored fish and a colorful salad.

MENU PLAN

1 Cook rice for Mahimahi in Grape Sauce; keep warm.

2 Complete step 1 of Asparagus-Tomato Salad.

3 Prepare Mahimahi in Grape Sauce.

4 While fish cooks, complete step 2 of Asparagus-Tomato Salad.

5 Prepare Amaretto Breeze just before serving.

Mahimahi in Grape Sauce (page 44)

Mahimahi in Grape Sauce

⅓ cup all-purpose flour
¼ teaspoon salt
⅛ teaspoon pepper
4 (½-pound) mahimahi fillets

¼ cup butter or margarine
1½ cups seedless green grapes,
    halved
½ cup dry vermouth
Hot cooked rice

1 Combine first 3 ingredients; dredge fillets in flour mixture.

2 Melt butter in a large skillet; add fillets, and cook 5 minutes on each side or until fish is almost done. Add grapes and vermouth; cover and simmer 3 minutes or until fish flakes easily when tested with a fork. Serve with rice. Yield: 4 servings.

Asparagus-Tomato Salad

1 pound fresh asparagus*

8 romaine lettuce leaves
12 cherry tomatoes, sliced
⅓ cup commercial reduced-
    calorie Italian salad
    dressing
¼ cup freshly grated Parmesan
    cheese

1 Snap off tough ends of asparagus; remove scales from stalks with a knife or vegetable peeler, if desired. Arrange asparagus in a steamer basket over boiling water; cover and steam 6 minutes. Plunge asparagus into ice water to stop the cooking process; drain.

2 Arrange lettuce leaves on individual salad plates; arrange asparagus spears and tomato on lettuce leaves. Drizzle salads with dressing, and sprinkle with Parmesan cheese. Yield: 4 servings.

*Substitute 1(16-ounce) can asparagus spears, drained, for fresh asparagus, if desired.

Amaretto Breeze

PREP: 8 MINUTES

1½ **quarts vanilla ice cream**
⅓ **cup amaretto**
⅓ **cup brandy**

1 Combine half of each ingredient in container of an electric blender; cover and process until smooth, stopping once to scrape down sides. Pour mixture into 2 glasses.

2 Repeat procedure with remaining half of each ingredient. Serve immediately. Yield: 4 cups.

To save time, prepare Amaretto Breeze ahead, and freeze it in a large container. Just before serving, process again in the blender to liquefy.

Amaretto Breeze

FESTIVE FAMILY SUPPER

Steak Parmesan

Cream Cheese and Onion Mashed Potatoes

Steamed Fresh Broccoli

Decadent Mud Pie

Serves 4

GROCERIES NEEDED

Check staples: vegetable oil, salt, pepper, milk, egg

- Fresh broccoli
- ⅓ cup chopped green onions
- 1 cup pizza sauce
- 1 (7¾-ounce) package instant mashed potato flakes
- ½ cup fine, dry breadcrumbs
- 1 (9-ounce) graham cracker crust (10-inch diameter)
- Blanched slivered almonds
- 1 (11¾-ounce) jar hot fudge sauce
- 4 cubed sirloin steaks (about 1 pound)
- 1 (8-ounce) package cream cheese
- ½ cup freshly grated Parmesan cheese
- Frozen whipped topping
- ½ gallon coffee ice cream

EQUIPMENT NEEDED

- Large skillet
- 8-inch square baking dish
- Steamer basket
- Heavy saucepan

Weeknight suppers don't have to be dull. You can serve a festive family pleaser any night. Add a vase of flowers and brightly colored napkins to the table for an unexpected lively touch.

MENU PLAN

1 Complete step 1 of Decadent Mud Pie one day ahead; freeze.

2 Prepare Steak Parmesan.

3 While steaks bake, steam broccoli; keep warm.

4 Prepare Cream Cheese and Onion Mashed Potatoes.

5 Sprinkle cheese over Steak Parmesan.

6 Complete step 2 of Decadent Mud Pie just before serving.

Decadent Mud Pie (page 49)

Steak Parmesan (below), Cream Cheese and Onion Mashed Potatoes (facing page)

Steak Parmesan

PREP: 11 MINUTES; COOK: 26 MINUTES

½ cup fine, dry breadcrumbs
½ cup freshly grated Parmesan
    cheese, divided
1 large egg, lightly beaten
1 tablespoon water
⅛ teaspoon pepper
4 cubed sirloin steaks (about
    1 pound)

¼ cup vegetable oil
1 cup pizza sauce

1 Combine breadcrumbs and ¼ cup Parmesan cheese. Combine egg, water, and pepper. Dip steaks in egg mixture; then dredge steaks in breadcrumb mixture.

2 Brown steaks in hot oil in a large skillet over medium heat 3 minutes on each side. Arrange steaks in an 8-inch square baking dish; top with pizza sauce. Bake at 325° for 20 minutes or until done. Remove steaks from oven, and sprinkle with remaining ¼ cup Parmesan cheese. Yield: 4 servings.

Cream Cheese and Onion Mashed Potatoes

PREP: 10 MINUTES; COOK: 5 MINUTES

3½ cups water
1 cup milk
1 (7¾-ounce) package instant
    mashed potato flakes

1 (8-ounce) package cream
    cheese, cubed and softened
⅓ cup chopped green onions
1 teaspoon salt
¼ teaspoon pepper

1 Combine water and milk in a heavy saucepan; bring to a boil. Remove pan from heat; stir in packets of potato flakes. (Reserve seasoning mix packets for another use.)

2 Add cream cheese and remaining ingredients to potato mixture, stirring until blended. Serve immediately. Yield: 4 servings.

Decadent Mud Pie

PREP: 20 MINUTES

1 (11¾-ounce) jar hot fudge
    sauce, heated and divided
1 (9-ounce) graham cracker crust
    (10-inch diameter)
½ gallon coffee ice cream,
    softened

Frozen whipped topping, thawed
Blanched slivered almonds,
    toasted

1 Spread ⅓ cup fudge sauce evenly over bottom of crust. Spread ice cream over fudge sauce; cover and freeze until firm.

2 Let pie stand at room temperature 5 minutes. Cut into wedges. Top each serving with remaining fudge sauce, whipped topping, and almonds. Serve immediately. Yield: one 10-inch pie.

FYI

Heat the hot fudge sauce in the microwave. Just remove the lid from the jar, and microwave at HIGH 1 minute, stirring once.

ALL-AMERICAN FARE

All-American Meat Loaves

Parmesan Potatoes   Spinach Salad

Lemon Fluff Pie

Serves 4

GROCERIES NEEDED

Check staples: ketchup, prepared mustard, sugar, brown sugar, salt, pepper, seasoned salt, seasoned pepper, garlic powder, milk, eggs, butter or margarine

Optional garnishes: lemons for zest and slices, fresh mint sprigs

- 3 large baking potatoes (about 2 pounds)
- 2 medium onions
- ½ cup chopped green pepper
- Makings for spinach salad
- 2 tablespoons prepared horseradish
- 1 (3-ounce) package lemon-flavored gelatin
- 1 (9-ounce) graham cracker crust (10-inch diameter)
- ¾ cup quick-cooking oats
- 2 pounds ground chuck
- 1 (8-ounce) carton lemon yogurt
- ½ cup grated Parmesan cheese
- 1 lemon
- 1 (8-ounce) container frozen whipped topping

EQUIPMENT NEEDED

- Broiler pan with rack
- 2-quart baking dish

Advanced preparation pays off with this weeknight menu your family will love. And you'll get a bonus: four meat loaves to freeze for a headstart on another meal.

MENU PLAN

1 Make Lemon Fluff Pie the day before.

2 Complete step 1 of All-American Meat Loaves.

3 While meat loaves bake, prepare spinach salad; chill.

4 Prepare Parmesan Potatoes.

5 Complete step 2 of All-American Meat Loaves.

All-American Meat Loaf, spinach salad, Parmesan Potatoes (Recipes begin on following page.)

All-American Meat Loaves

PREP: 10 MINUTES; BAKE: 45 MINUTES

FYI

Chop the onion for both the meat loaf and the potatoes at one time. Wrap any leftover meat loaves tightly, and freeze up to two months for a headstart on another meal.

2 large eggs, lightly beaten
2 pounds ground chuck
1 medium onion, chopped
¾ cup quick-cooking oats, uncooked
½ cup ketchup
¼ cup milk
1 tablespoon prepared horseradish
1 teaspoon salt
¼ teaspoon pepper

½ cup ketchup
3 tablespoons brown sugar
1 tablespoon prepared horseradish
2 teaspoons prepared mustard

1 Combine first 9 ingredients; shape mixture into 8 (4- x 2½-inch) loaves. Place loaves on a lightly greased rack of a broiler pan. Bake, uncovered, at 400° for 40 minutes.

2 Combine ½ cup ketchup and remaining 3 ingredients. Remove pan from oven; pour ketchup mixture over meat loaves. Bake 5 additional minutes. Yield: 8 servings.

Parmesan Potatoes

PREP: 12 MINUTES; MICROWAVE: 13 MINUTES

¼ cup butter or margarine
½ cup grated Parmesan cheese
½ cup chopped green pepper
⅓ cup chopped onion
½ teaspoon seasoned salt
½ teaspoon seasoned pepper
¼ teaspoon garlic powder
3 large baking potatoes (about 2 pounds), peeled and cut into ¼-inch-thick slices

1 Place butter in a 2-quart baking dish; microwave at HIGH 30 seconds or until butter melts. Stir in Parmesan cheese and next 5 ingredients. Add sliced potato, and toss gently to coat.

2 Cover baking dish tightly with heavy-duty plastic wrap; fold back a small edge of wrap to allow steam to escape. Microwave potato at HIGH 13 to 15 minutes or until potato is tender, stirring at 5-minute intervals. Yield: 4 servings.

Lemon Fluff Pie

Lemon Fluff Pie

PREP: 13 MINUTES; CHILL: 3½ HOURS

1 (3-ounce) package lemon-
    flavored gelatin
1½ tablespoons sugar
1 cup boiling water
¼ cup plus 2 tablespoons cold
    water
2 tablespoons fresh lemon juice

1 (8-ounce) carton lemon yogurt
1 (8-ounce) container frozen
    whipped topping, thawed
2 teaspoons grated lemon rind
    (optional)
1 (9-ounce) graham cracker crust
    (10-inch diameter)
Garnishes: lemon slices, lemon
    zest, fresh mint sprigs

1 Combine gelatin, sugar, and boiling water, stirring 2 minutes or until gelatin dissolves. Stir in cold water and lemon juice. Chill 30 minutes or until mixture is the consistency of unbeaten egg white.

2 Fold yogurt, whipped topping, and, if desired, lemon rind into gelatin mixture; spoon into crust. Chill at least 3 hours. Garnish, if desired. Yield: one 10-inch pie.

Note: Spoon filling mixture into 12 single-serve graham cracker crusts, if desired.

WEEKNIGHT SPAGHETTI SUPPER

Meaty Spaghetti

Tossed Green Salad with Vinaigrette Dressing

Quick Garlic Bread

Hot Fudge Sundaes

Serves 6

GROCERIES NEEDED

Check staples: Dijon mustard, olive oil, sugar, dried parsley flakes, dried oregano, dried basil, garlic powder, paprika, salt, butter or margarine

- 1 medium onion
- Makings for tossed green salad
- 2 (6-ounce) cans tomato paste
- 1 (28-ounce) can whole tomatoes
- 1 (8-ounce) can tomato sauce
- Spaghetti
- ¼ cup white wine vinegar
- 1 teaspoon lemon juice
- Hot fudge sauce
- Sundae toppings
- 1½ pounds ground chuck
- 1 (16-ounce) loaf sliced French bread
- Grated Parmesan cheese
- Vanilla ice cream

EQUIPMENT NEEDED

- 2 Dutch ovens
- Jar with lid
- Baking sheet

Serve this menu on nights when time is short and appetites are hearty. Supper will be a snap because it comes together quickly.

MENU PLAN

1 Complete steps 1 and 2 of Meaty Spaghetti.

2 While spaghetti sauce simmers, cook spaghetti; keep warm.

3 Prepare Vinaigrette Dressing and tossed green salad.

4 Prepare Quick Garlic Bread.

5 Prepare hot fudge sundaes just before serving.

Meaty Spaghetti (page 56)

Meaty Spaghetti

PREP: 5 MINUTES; COOK: 30 MINUTES

FYI

Put on the water to boil for the spaghetti while the meat browns. Cover the pot to hold in the heat so the water will come to a boil faster. Salt the water when you add the pasta, and cook the pasta uncovered.

1½ pounds ground chuck
1 medium onion, chopped

1 (28-ounce) can whole tomatoes, undrained and chopped
2 (6-ounce) cans tomato paste
1 (8-ounce) can tomato sauce
2 teaspoons sugar
1½ teaspoons dried oregano
1½ teaspoons dried basil
¾ teaspoon garlic powder

Hot cooked spaghetti
Grated Parmesan cheese

1 Cook ground chuck and onion in a Dutch oven until meat is browned, stirring until it crumbles. Drain.

2 Stir chopped tomato and next 6 ingredients into meat mixture; cook over medium heat 20 minutes, stirring occasionally.

3 Serve sauce over hot cooked spaghetti; sprinkle with Parmesan cheese. Yield: 6 servings.

Vinaigrette Dressing

PREP: 5 MINUTES

½ cup olive oil
¼ cup white wine vinegar
1 teaspoon lemon juice
½ teaspoon Dijon mustard
⅛ teaspoon salt
⅛ teaspoon garlic powder

1 Combine all ingredients in a jar. Cover tightly, and shake vigorously. Serve dressing over a green salad. Yield: ¾ cup.

Quick Garlic Bread

PREP: **9 MINUTES**; BROIL: **4 MINUTES**

¼ cup butter or margarine, softened
1 tablespoon grated Parmesan cheese
½ teaspoon dried parsley flakes
⅛ teaspoon garlic powder
⅛ teaspoon paprika
1 (16-ounce) loaf sliced French bread

1 Combine first 5 ingredients; spread mixture on 1 side of each bread slice. Place bread slices on an ungreased baking sheet.

2 Broil 5½ inches from heat (with electric oven door partially opened) 4 to 5 minutes or until bread is lightly toasted. Yield: 1 loaf.

Spread the topping on the bread ahead; wrap the loaf tightly, and chill. Broil the bread just before serving.

Quick Garlic Bread

DOWN-HOME DELICIOUS

Mustard-Apricot Pork Chops

Basil-Cheese Potatoes

Bean and Tomato Skillet

Ice Cream

Serves 4

GROCERIES NEEDED

Check staples: Dijon mustard, sugar, vegetable oil, dried basil, salt, pepper, bay leaf, butter or margarine

- 3 green onions
- 2 large baking potatoes
- 2 small onions
- 2 medium tomatoes
- ⅓ cup apricot preserves
- 1 teaspoon lemon juice
- 4 (¾-inch-thick) pork loin chops
- 2 tablespoons grated Parmesan cheese
- 1 (9-ounce) package frozen whole green beans
- Ice cream

EQUIPMENT NEEDED

- Small saucepan
- Broiler pan with rack
- Basting brush
- 11- x 7- x 1½-inch baking dish
- Large skillet with lid

Time may be short, but never too short to prepare this down-home supper. It features the convenience of the microwave, as well as the speed of cooking on the stove top and with the broiler.

MENU PLAN

1 Complete step 1 of Mustard-Apricot Pork Chops.

2 Prepare Basil-Cheese Potatoes.

3 Complete step 1 of Bean and Tomato Skillet.

4 Compete step 2 of Mustard-Apricot Pork Chops.

5 While pork chops broil, complete step 2 of Bean and Tomato Skillet.

6 Scoop ice cream to serve for dessert.

Mustard-Apricot Pork Chops, Basil-Cheese Potatoes, Bean and Tomato Skillet (Recipes begin on following page.)

Mustard-Apricot Pork Chops

PREP: 3 MINUTES; COOK: 15 MINUTES

Broil the pork chops while the potatoes and the beans cook.

⅓ cup apricot preserves
2 tablespoons Dijon mustard

4 (¾-inch-thick) pork loin chops, trimmed
3 green onions, chopped

1 Combine preserves and mustard in a small saucepan; heat until preserves melt, stirring occasionally. Set aside.

2 Place pork chops on greased rack of a broiler pan; broil chops 5½ inches from heat (with electric oven door partially opened) 5 minutes. Brush chops with half of preserves mixture; turn and broil 5 additional minutes. Brush chops with remaining preserves mixture; broil 2 additional minutes. Sprinkle with green onions. Yield: 4 servings.

Basil-Cheese Potatoes

PREP: 5 MINUTES; MICROWAVE: 14 MINUTES

1 teaspoon butter or margarine, melted
1 teaspoon lemon juice
2 large baking potatoes, halved lengthwise
2 tablespoons grated Parmesan cheese
½ teaspoon dried basil
¼ teaspoon pepper

1 Combine butter and lemon juice; brush over cut surfaces of potato halves. Combine Parmesan cheese, basil, and pepper; sprinkle over cut surfaces of potato halves.

2 Place potato halves, cut sides up, in an 11- x 7- x 1½-inch baking dish; cover dish with wax paper. Microwave at HIGH 14 to 16 minutes, giving dish a half-turn after 7 minutes. Let stand 2 minutes before serving. Yield: 4 servings.

Bean and Tomato Skillet

PREP: 10 MINUTES; COOK: 17 MINUTES

1 tablespoon vegetable oil
1 (9-ounce) package frozen whole
    green beans
2 small onions, sliced
1 teaspoon sugar
½ teaspoon salt
1 bay leaf

2 medium tomatoes, cut into
    chunks

1 Heat oil in a large skillet over medium heat until hot. Stir in beans and next 4 ingredients. Cover and cook over medium heat 10 minutes; remove and discard bay leaf.

2 Scatter tomato chunks over mixture; cover and cook 7 minutes. Yield: 4 servings.

Bean and Tomato Skillet

SPECIAL-OCCASION DINNER

Buttermilk-Pecan Chicken

Lemon Rice   *Tossed Green Salad*

Cantaloupe Sundaes

Serves 8

GROCERIES NEEDED

Check staples: all-purpose flour, cornstarch, vegetable oil, vegetable cooking spray, salt, pepper, paprika, egg, butter or margarine

Optional garnishes: fresh parsley, lemon slices

- 2 cantaloupes
- 2 cloves garlic
- 2 lemons
- 1 medium onion
- ½ cup chopped fresh parsley
- Makings for tossed green salad
- 2 cups uncooked long-grain rice
- ¾ cup fine, dry breadcrumbs
- 1 cup ground pecans
- ¼ cup coarsely chopped pecans
- 4 chicken-flavored bouillon cubes
- 8 skinned and boned chicken breast halves
- 1 cup buttermilk
- 1 quart vanilla ice cream
- 1 (10-ounce) package frozen raspberries

EQUIPMENT NEEDED

- Broiler pan with rack
- Large saucepan with lid
- Medium saucepan

Celebrate a family birthday, job promotion, or graduation with this lavish menu. A fantastic dinner doesn't have to mean extra time in the kitchen—but the honoree will think you spent hours preparing it.

MENU PLAN

1 Complete step 1 of Cantaloupe Sundaes. Peel cantaloupes, and cut into wedges; chill.

2 Prepare Buttermilk-Pecan Chicken.

3 While chicken bakes, prepare Lemon Rice; keep warm.

4 While rice cooks, prepare tossed salad.

5 Assemble Cantaloupe Sundaes just before serving.

Buttermilk-Pecan Chicken, Lemon Rice (page 64)

Buttermilk-Pecan Chicken

PREP: 15 MINUTES; BAKE: 30 MINUTES

FYI

Use a food processor to prepare the pecans, onions, and parsley for this menu.

1 cup buttermilk
1 large egg, lightly beaten

1 cup ground pecans
¾ cup fine, dry breadcrumbs
2 teaspoons paprika
1½ teaspoons salt
⅛ teaspoon pepper

8 skinned and boned chicken breast halves
½ cup all-purpose flour

Vegetable cooking spray
⅓ cup butter or margarine, melted
¼ cup coarsely chopped pecans

1 Combine buttermilk and egg.

2 Combine ground pecans and next 4 ingredients.

3 Dredge chicken in flour. Dip in buttermilk mixture; drain. Dredge chicken in pecan mixture.

4 Place chicken on rack of a broiler pan coated with cooking spray. Drizzle chicken with melted butter; sprinkle with chopped pecans. Bake, uncovered, at 350° for 30 minutes or until done. Yield 8 servings.

Lemon Rice

PREP: 8 MINUTES; COOK: 23 MINUTES

1 medium onion, chopped
2 cloves garlic, minced
1 tablespoon vegetable oil

4 cups water
2 cups long-grain rice, uncooked
1 teaspoon grated lemon rind
3 tablespoons lemon juice
4 chicken-flavored bouillon cubes

½ cup chopped fresh parsley
Garnishes: fresh parsley sprigs, lemon slices

1 Cook onion and garlic in hot oil in a large saucepan over medium-high heat, stirring constantly, 3 minutes or until tender.

2 Add water and next 4 ingredients; bring to a boil. Cover, reduce heat, and simmer 20 to 25 minutes or until rice is tender and liquid is absorbed.

3 Stir parsley into rice mixture. Garnish, if desired. Yield: 8 servings.

Cantaloupe Sundaes

PREP: 15 MINUTES; COOK: 3 MINUTES

2 teaspoons cornstarch
2 tablespoons water
1 (10-ounce) package frozen
    raspberries, thawed

2 cantaloupes, peeled and cut into
    4 wedges each
1 quart vanilla ice cream

1 Combine cornstarch and water in a medium saucepan over medium-high heat. Add raspberries; bring to a boil. Cook, stirring constantly, 1 minute. Cool.

2 To serve, fill each cantaloupe wedge with a scoop of ice cream. Spoon raspberry mixture over ice cream. Yield: 8 servings.

Cantaloupe Sundae

Fuss-free is the key with these 10 menus. The selections are about as simple as meal preparation gets: one recipe to prepare, one or two suggestions for quick-fix or purchased side dishes, and a commercial dessert. And

30 MINUTE MEALS

you have our test kitchen staff's seal of approval that lunch or dinner will be on the table in 30 minutes or less. In fact, this chapter is a winner with our staff because of how hurriedly we usually have to get dinner on the table.

"Fit for Company" menu features Shrimp and Tortellini, sliced tomatoes, and steamed asparagus. (page 69)

Oven-Baked Catfish

Fish in a Flash

Oven-Baked Catfish

French Fries

Coleslaw

Citrus Fruit Cups

Serves 4

Oven-Baked Catfish

PREP: 6 MINUTES; BAKE: 10 MINUTES

FYI

Frozen french fries and deli coleslaw are ready-to-go side dishes. Line the bottom of the broiler pan with aluminum foil for easy cleanup. Purchase refrigerated citrus sections for the simplest dessert ever.

¼ **cup butter or margarine, melted**
2 **tablespoons lemon juice**
4 **farm-raised catfish fillets (about 2 pounds)**
1 **cup Italian-seasoned breadcrumbs**

Lemon wedges (optional)
Tartar sauce (optional)
Cocktail sauce (optional)

1 Combine butter and lemon juice in a small shallow dish. Dredge fish in breadcrumbs; dip in butter mixture. Dredge again in breadcrumbs.

2 Place fish on a lightly greased rack of a broiler pan. Broil fish 5½ inches from heat (with electric oven door partially opened) 10 minutes or until fish flakes easily when tested with a fork. Serve fish with lemon wedges, tartar sauce, and cocktail sauce, if desired. Yield: 4 servings.

Fit for Company

Shrimp and Tortellini

Steamed Asparagus

Sliced Tomatoes

Dinner Rolls

Sorbet

Serves 4

Shrimp and Tortellini

Shrimp and Tortellini

PREP: 12 MINUTES; COOK: 10 MINUTES

2 pounds unpeeled medium-size fresh shrimp

1 (9-ounce) package fresh cheese-filled tortellini, uncooked

⅓ cup butter or margarine
1 shallot, minced
2 tablespoons chopped fresh basil
½ cup freshly grated Parmesan cheese
Garnish: fresh basil sprigs

1 Peel shrimp, and devein, if desired. Set aside.

2 Cook tortellini according to package directions; drain.

3 While tortellini cooks, melt butter in a large skillet over medium-high heat. Add shrimp, shallot, and chopped basil to skillet. Cook 4 to 5 minutes, stirring constantly, until shrimp turn pink. Add tortellini and Parmesan cheese; toss gently. Garnish, if desired. Yield: 4 servings.

FYI

Choose asparagus stalks that are uniform in size to ensure even cooking. Steam the asparagus while the tortellini cooks. Save time and nutrients by leaving the peel on the tomatoes.

Stir-Fry Beef and Asparagus

Dinner from The Wok

Stir-Fry Beef and Asparagus

Fresh Fruit Salad

Frozen Yogurt

Serves 4

Stir-Fry Beef and Asparagus

PREP: 10 MINUTES; MARINATE: 10 MINUTES; COOK: 10 MINUTES

FYI

The steak will be easier to slice if you freeze it 30 minutes before cutting. Or you can buy cut stir-fry beef. Select cut fruit in the produce section for the salad, and top it with commercial poppy seed dressing.

2 teaspoons cornstarch
2 tablespoons dry sherry
2 tablespoons soy sauce
1 pound boneless sirloin steak, sliced diagonally across grain into thin strips

1 pound fresh asparagus

1½ tablespoons vegetable oil

3 tablespoons beef broth
1 teaspoon cornstarch
1 tablespoon dry sherry
1 tablespoon soy sauce
Hot cooked rice

1 Combine first 3 ingredients; pour over steak. Marinate 10 minutes.

2 Snap off tough ends of asparagus. Remove scales, if desired. Cut stalks diagonally into 1-inch pieces.

3 Drain steak. Pour oil around top of preheated wok; heat at medium-high (375°) for 2 minutes. Add steak; stir-fry 4 minutes. Remove from wok.

4 Add asparagus and broth to wok; bring to a boil. Cover and simmer 3 minutes. Combine 1 teaspoon cornstarch, 1 tablespoon sherry, and 1 tablespoon soy sauce; add to wok. Cook, stirring constantly, until thickened. Stir in steak. Serve over rice. Yield: 4 servings.

Spotlight Steak Tonight

Chicken-Fried Steak

Mashed Potatoes

Peas and Carrots

Biscuits

Pound Cake

Serves 4

Chicken-Fried Steak

Chicken-Fried Steak

PREP: 5 MINUTES; COOK: 25 MINUTES

¼ cup all-purpose flour
½ teaspoon salt
½ teaspoon pepper
1 pound cubed beef steaks
1 large egg, lightly beaten
2 tablespoons milk
1 cup saltine cracker crumbs

Vegetable oil

3 tablespoons all-purpose flour
1¼ cups chicken broth
½ cup milk
Dash of Worcestershire sauce
Dash of hot sauce
Additional pepper

1 Combine first 3 ingredients; sprinkle over both sides of steaks. Combine egg and 2 tablespoons milk. Dip steaks in egg mixture; dredge in cracker crumbs.

2 Pour oil to depth of ½ inch into a skillet. Brown steaks over medium heat. Cover, reduce heat, and cook 15 minutes or until tender, turning occasionally. Drain on paper towels.

3 Reserve 3 tablespoons drippings in skillet; stir in 3 tablespoons flour. Cook over medium heat, stirring constantly, 1 minute. Gradually add broth and next 3 ingredients; cook, stirring constantly, until thickened. Serve steaks with gravy and additional pepper. Yield: 4 servings.

FYI

If you're short on time, prepare instant potato flakes for the mashed potatoes. Use a biscuit mix or canned biscuits for a quick bread. Frozen peas and carrots are brighter and taste fresher than canned.

Quick-and-Easy Chili

Quick-and-Easy Chili

Coleslaw

Corn Sticks

Brownies

Serves 4

Quick-and-Easy Chili

PREP: 7 MINUTES; COOK: 15 MINUTES

FYI

Save time by using a corn muffin mix to prepare the corn sticks. Bake the brownies in advance, or buy some at the bakery.

1 pound ground chuck

2 (15¼-ounce) cans kidney beans, undrained

1 (14½-ounce) can whole tomatoes, undrained and chopped

1 (10-ounce) can diced tomatoes and green chiles, undrained

1 (1¾-ounce) envelope chili seasoning mix

1½ cups water

1 tablespoon instant onion soup mix

Shredded sharp Cheddar cheese
Sour cream

1 Brown ground chuck in a Dutch oven, stirring until it crumbles; drain.

2 Add beans and next 5 ingredients to beef in Dutch oven; bring to a boil. Reduce heat to medium, and simmer, uncovered, 15 minutes, stirring occasionally.

3 Ladle chili into bowls; sprinkle with cheese, and dollop with sour cream. Yield: 9 cups.

Dinner On-the-Double

Taco-Topped Potatoes

Shredded Iceberg Lettuce
With Guacamole

Vanilla Ice Cream
With Chocolate Sauce

Serves 4

Taco-Topped Potatoes

Taco-Topped Potatoes

PREP: 5 MINUTES; COOK: 25 MINUTES

4 large baking potatoes (about
    2¾ pounds)

1 pound ground chuck
½ cup chopped onion
¾ cup water
1 (1¼-ounce) package taco
    seasoning mix
1 cup taco sauce

1 cup (4 ounces) shredded
    Monterey Jack cheese
    with peppers

1 Scrub potatoes; prick several times with a fork. Place potatoes 1 inch apart on a microwave-safe rack or on paper towels. Microwave at HIGH 14 to 17 minutes, rearranging once; let stand 2 minutes.

2 Cook beef and onion in a skillet, stirring until beef crumbles; drain. Stir water and seasoning mix into meat mixture; bring to a boil. Reduce heat; simmer, uncovered, 5 minutes or until liquid evaporates, stirring occasionally. Add taco sauce; cook 1 minute.

3 Cut an X to within ½ inch of bottoms of potatoes. Squeeze potatoes to open; fluff with a fork. Spoon meat mixture onto potatoes; sprinkle with cheese. Yield: 4 servings.

FYI

Use your food processor to shred the cheese and to chop the onion. Pick up guacamole from the frozen food or refrigerated section of the supermarket.

Barbecued Franks

Supper Before The Game

Barbecued Franks

Potato Chips

Carrot and Celery Sticks

Cookies

Serves 8

Barbecued Franks

PREP: 8 MINUTES; COOK: 20 MINUTES

FYI

Keep ready-to-eat carrot and celery sticks in the refrigerator. They make an easy side dish for a menu like this and a quick, healthy snack for any time.

¾ **cup chopped onion**
½ **cup chopped green pepper**
¼ **cup chopped celery**
1 **tablespoon butter or margarine, melted**

¾ **cup ketchup**
½ **cup water**
1½ **tablespoons sugar**
2 **tablespoons lemon juice**
1½ **tablespoons white vinegar**
2 **teaspoons Worcestershire sauce**
¾ **teaspoon dry mustard**

8 **frankfurters**
8 **hot dog buns**

1 Cook first 3 ingredients in butter in a large skillet over medium-high heat, stirring constantly, until tender.

2 Stir ketchup and next 6 ingredients into vegetable mixture. Cook over medium heat 10 minutes, stirring occasionally.

3 Add frankfurters to sauce; simmer 5 minutes or until frankfurters are thoroughly heated. To serve, place frankfurters in buns, and top with sauce. Yield: 8 servings.

Cajun Family Favorite

Sausage Jambalaya

Iceberg Lettuce Wedges
With Salad Dressing

French Bread

Angel Food Cake
With Strawberries

Serves 6

Sausage Jambalaya

Sausage Jambalaya

PREP: 10 MINUTES; COOK: 15 MINUTES

2 large packages boil-in-bag rice,
   uncooked

1 pound smoked sausage, cut into
   ¼-inch diagonal slices
1⅓ cups chopped cooked ham
2 stalks celery, chopped
2 cloves garlic, minced
1 medium onion, chopped

1 (14½-ounce) can ready-
   to-serve beef broth
½ teaspoon black pepper
½ teaspoon ground red pepper

1 Prepare rice according to package
directions. Drain and keep warm.

2 While rice cooks, combine sausage
and next 4 ingredients in a Dutch
oven. Cook over medium-high heat,
stirring constantly, until sausage is
browned.

3 Add broth, black pepper, and red
pepper to Dutch oven; bring mixture to a boil. Reduce heat, and simmer, uncovered, 5 minutes, stirring
occasionally. Stir in cooked rice.
Yield: 6 servings.

FYI

*Leftover ham is perfect
for jambalaya. Make a
quick salad by topping
large lettuce wedges
with commercial
salad dressing.*

Spicy White Bean Soup

Spicy White Bean Soup

PREP: 5 MINUTES; COOK: 25 MINUTES

FYI

While the soup simmers, bake a pan of cornbread using a packaged mix.

1 large onion, chopped
2 tablespoons butter or
   margarine, melted

2 (15½-ounce) cans Great
   Northern beans, drained
2 (15½-ounce) cans yellow
   hominy, drained
2 (14½-ounce) cans chili-style
   chopped tomatoes,
   undrained
2 (14½-ounce) cans ready-
   to-serve vegetable broth
1 teaspoon sugar
½ teaspoon ground cumin
½ teaspoon ground red pepper
¼ teaspoon ground cloves
2 tablespoons chopped fresh
   cilantro

1 Cook onion in butter in a large Dutch oven over medium-high heat, stirring constantly, until tender.

2 Add beans and remaining ingredients to Dutch oven. Bring to a boil, stirring occasionally. Reduce heat, and simmer, uncovered, 15 minutes, stirring occasionally. Yield: 3 quarts.

Skillet Dinner

Skillet Chicken and Rice

Steamed Carrots

Tossed Green Salad

Lemon Sherbet

Serves 4

Skillet Chicken and Rice

Skillet Chicken and Rice

PREP: 5 MINUTES; COOK: 22 MINUTES

1⅓ cups milk

1 (10¾-ounce) can cream of
mushroom soup, undiluted

1 (6-ounce) package quick long-
grain and wild rice mix
(including seasoning
packet), uncooked

4 skinned and boned chicken
breast halves

1 tablespoon butter or
margarine, melted

1 Combine milk, soup, rice mix, and seasoning packet; set aside.

2 Cook chicken in butter in a large skillet over medium-high heat 5 minutes on each side. Pour rice mixture over chicken; bring to a boil. Cover, reduce heat, and simmer 12 minutes or until chicken is done and liquid is absorbed. Yield: 4 servings.

FYI

Speed up salad preparation by purchasing a prepackaged gourmet salad mix. Cut a few cherry tomatoes in half to add color, and drizzle salad with Italian dressing.

Company Salad with
Raspberry Vinaigrette (page 127)

Quick
RECIPES

Whether the occasion is casual or formal, the crowd large or small, we've got a quick-to-fix appetizer to suit your needs. You'll find **MEATY CHEESE DIP** for the football fans, **ORIENTAL CHICKEN APPETIZERS** for a

*A*PPETIZERS & BEVERAGES

holiday party, and **WALNUT-ROQUEFORT SPREAD** for a sophisticated prelude to dinner. And don't forget the beverages. They range from eye-opening **OKLAHOMA SUNRISE** to enjoy in the morning to a warming cup of **HOT BUTTERED LEMONADE** to serve fireside.

Clockwise from bottom: Black Bean Salsa (page 82), Lemon-Lime Margaritas (page 94), Easy Guacamole (page 82)

Easy Guacamole

PREP: 7 MINUTES

Use a pastry blender to mash ripe avocados for chunky guacamole.

2 medium-size ripe avocados,
  peeled and mashed
¼ cup picante sauce
1½ teaspoons lemon juice
½ teaspoon garlic salt

1 Combine all ingredients. Serve dip with tortilla chips. Yield: 1½ cups.

Black Bean Salsa

PREP: 10 MINUTES; CHILL: 2 HOURS

1 (15-ounce) can black beans,
  rinsed and drained
1 cup thick-and-chunky salsa
3 tablespoons chopped fresh
  cilantro
2 tablespoons lime juice
½ teaspoon ground cumin

1 Combine all ingredients. Cover and chill at least 2 hours. Serve with tortilla chips. Yield: 2¼ cups.

One-Minute Salsa

PREP: 1 MINUTE

1 (14½-ounce) can stewed
  tomatoes, undrained
1 (10-ounce) can diced tomatoes
  and green chiles, undrained
½ teaspoon garlic salt
½ teaspoon pepper

1 Combine all ingredients in container of an electric blender; cover and process 15 seconds or until smooth. Transfer mixture to a bowl; cover and chill, if desired. Serve with tortilla chips. Yield: 2¾ cups.

Pub Fondue

PREP: 2 MINUTES; COOK: 10 MINUTES

1 (10¾-ounce) can Cheddar
   cheese soup, undiluted
¾ cup beer
2 cups (8 ounces) shredded mild
   Cheddar cheese
2 teaspoons prepared mustard
1 teaspoon Worcestershire sauce

1 Combine soup and beer in a medium saucepan; bring to a boil over medium heat, stirring constantly. Gradually add cheese, stirring constantly until cheese melts. Stir in mustard and Worcestershire sauce.

2 Spoon mixture into a fondue pot or chafing dish; serve warm with French bread cubes. Yield: 2¾ cups.

FYI

Cheeses like Cheddar, Monterey Jack, and Swiss are easier to shred when cold. Next time you're shredding cheese for a recipe, shred extra to freeze for later use.

Swiss-Onion Dip

PREP: 5 MINUTES; BAKE: 25 MINUTES

1 (10-ounce) package frozen
   chopped onion, thawed
3 cups (12 ounces) shredded
   Swiss cheese
1 cup mayonnaise
1 tablespoon coarse-grained Dijon
   mustard
¼ teaspoon salt
⅛ teaspoon pepper

1 Press onion between layers of paper towels to remove excess moisture. Combine onion, cheese, and remaining ingredients; spoon mixture into an ungreased 1-quart baking dish.

2 Bake at 325° for 25 minutes or until lightly browned and bubbly. Serve warm with Melba rounds. Yield: 4 cups.

Meaty Cheese Dip

Meaty Cheese Dip

PREP: 3 MINUTES; COOK: 12 MINUTES

1 pound ground chuck
½ pound ground hot pork sausage

1 (2-pound) loaf process cheese
    spread, cubed*
1 (8-ounce) jar medium salsa
Garnish: large corn chip

1 Brown ground chuck and sausage in a large skillet, stirring until meat crumbles; drain.

2 Add cheese and salsa; cook over low heat, stirring constantly, until cheese melts. Garnish, if desired. Serve warm with large corn chips. Yield: 6 cups.

* Substitute 1 (2-pound) loaf Mexican process cheese spread, if desired.

Kahlúa-Pecan Brie

PREP: 10 MINUTES; BAKE: 5 MINUTES

1 (15-ounce) round Brie

½ cup chopped pecans, toasted
2½ tablespoons Kahlúa or other
    coffee-flavored liqueur
2 tablespoons brown sugar

1 Remove rind from top of cheese, cutting to within ½ inch of edge. Place on an oven-safe dish.

2 Combine pecans, Kahlúa, and brown sugar; spread over cheese. Bake at 350° for 5 minutes or just until soft. Serve immediately with gingersnaps or apple slices. Yield: 8 appetizer servings.

FYI

Put your microwave to use toasting pecans. Spread ½ cup pecans in a pieplate. Microwave at HIGH 3½ minutes, or microwave 1 cup for 4 to 5 minutes, stirring at 2-minute intervals.

Ham and Cheese Ball

PREP: 15 MINUTES; CHILL: 30 MINUTES

2 (8-ounce) packages cream
    cheese, softened
1 (2½-ounce) package thinly
    sliced ham, chopped
¼ cup commercial Italian salad
    dressing

¾ cup chopped pecans

1 Combine first 3 ingredients; cover and chill at least 30 minutes.

2 Shape mixture into a ball using a rubber spatula; roll cheese ball in chopped pecans. Serve with crackers. Yield: one 4-inch cheese ball.

Chicken-Curry Cheese Ball

PREP: 10 MINUTES; CHILL: 30 MINUTES

FYI

Two chicken breast halves, cooked and chopped, equal about one cup chicken. If you're short on time, purchase frozen chopped, cooked chicken.

1 (8-ounce) package cream cheese, softened
1 cup finely chopped cooked chicken
¾ cup finely chopped almonds, toasted
⅓ cup mayonnaise
2 tablespoons chutney
1 tablespoon curry powder

Chopped fresh parsley

1 Combine first 6 ingredients; cover and chill at least 30 minutes.

2 Shape mixture into a ball; roll in chopped parsley. Serve with crackers. Yield: one 4-inch cheese ball.

Mexican Cheese Spread

PREP: 13 MINUTES

2 cups (8 ounces) shredded sharp Cheddar cheese
½ cup sour cream
¼ cup butter or margarine, softened

2 green onions, chopped
1 (2-ounce) jar diced pimiento, drained
2 tablespoons chopped green chiles

1 Combine first 3 ingredients in a mixing bowl; beat at medium speed of an electric mixer until blended.

2 Stir in green onions, pimiento, and chiles. Cover and chill, if desired. Serve with crackers. Yield: 2 cups.

Curried Chutney Spread

PREP: 20 MINUTES; CHILL: 8 HOURS

2 (8-ounce) packages cream
    cheese, softened
¾ cup finely chopped pecans
½ cup chutney
1¼ teaspoons curry powder

Garnish: pecan halves

1 Combine first 4 ingredients in a mixing bowl; beat at medium speed of an electric mixer until blended.

2 Spoon mixture into a serving bowl; cover and chill at least 8 hours. Garnish, if desired. Serve with gingersnaps, apple slices, or crackers. Yield: 2½ cups.

FYI

Chop pecans in the food processor using the on/off pulsing method. Be careful not to overprocess, or you'll end up with ground pecans.

Curried Chutney Spread

Hearts of Palm Spread

PREP: **7** MINUTES; BAKE: **20** MINUTES

1 (14.4-ounce) can hearts of palm, drained and chopped
1 cup (4 ounces) shredded mozzarella cheese
¾ cup mayonnaise
½ cup grated Parmesan cheese
¼ cup sour cream
2 tablespoons minced green onions

1 Combine all ingredients; spoon mixture into a lightly greased 9-inch quiche dish or pieplate. Bake at 350° for 20 minutes or until hot and bubbly. Serve with crackers or Melba rounds. Yield: 2 cups.

Walnut-Roquefort Spread

PREP: **25** MINUTES; CHILL: **2** HOURS

1 envelope unflavored gelatin
½ cup cold water

1 (8-ounce) package cream cheese, softened
1½ ounces Roquefort cheese
¼ teaspoon salt
1 cup whipping cream

½ cup finely chopped walnuts

1 Sprinkle gelatin over cold water in a small saucepan; let stand 1 minute. Cook over low heat, stirring until gelatin dissolves (about 2 minutes).

2 Combine cream cheese, Roquefort cheese, and salt in a mixing bowl; beat at medium speed of an electric mixer until blended. Gradually add gelatin mixture; beat well. Add whipping cream, beating until mixture is fluffy. Pour mixture into a lightly oiled 4-cup mold. Cover and chill at least 2 hours.

3 Invert mold onto a serving plate; sprinkle with walnuts. Serve with crackers or fresh fruit. Yield: 4 cups.

Marinated Artichoke Hearts

PREP: 5 MINUTES; MARINATE: 8 HOURS

¼ cup olive oil
¼ cup white wine vinegar
⅛ teaspoon salt
⅛ teaspoon pepper
⅛ teaspoon dried parsley flakes
⅛ teaspoon dried oregano
⅛ teaspoon dried basil
⅛ teaspoon dried marjoram

1 (14-ounce) can quartered
   artichoke hearts, drained

1 Combine first 8 ingredients in a small jar; cover tightly, and shake vigorously.

2 Place artichokes in a single layer in a shallow dish; pour oil mixture over artichokes. Cover and marinate in refrigerator at least 8 hours, stirring occasionally. Drain before serving. Yield: 4 appetizer servings.

Stuffed Cherry Tomatoes

PREP: 27 MINUTES

36 large cherry tomatoes (about
   2 pints)

1 (8-ounce) package cream
   cheese, softened
3 to 4 tablespoons whipping
   cream
2 tablespoons chopped fresh
   chives
¼ teaspoon salt
¼ teaspoon ground white pepper

1 Cut top off each tomato; scoop out pulp, leaving shells intact. Discard pulp. Invert tomato shells onto paper towels to drain.

2 Combine cream cheese and remaining 4 ingredients in a mixing bowl; beat at medium speed of an electric mixer until mixture is creamy, adding enough whipping cream to make a slightly soft mixture. Pipe or spoon mixture into tomato shells. Yield: 3 dozen.

F*Y*I

Soften one 8-ounce package of cream cheese quickly. Just unwrap the block, and place it on a microwave-safe plate. Then microwave at MEDIUM (50% power) 1 minute or just until softened.

Sesame Cheese Wafers

Sesame Cheese Wafers

PREP: 15 MINUTES; CHILL: 30 MINUTES; BAKE: 8 MINUTES

½ (15-ounce) package
    refrigerated piecrusts
1½ cups (6 ounces) shredded
    sharp Cheddar cheese
½ cup sesame seeds, toasted
½ teaspoon ground red pepper

1 to 2 teaspoons ice water

1 Position knife blade in food processor bowl; add first 4 ingredients. Cover and process 30 seconds.

2 Add ice water (1 teaspoon at a time) through food chute with processor running; process just until dough begins to form a ball and leaves sides of bowl. Cover and chill 30 minutes.

3 Shape dough into 1-inch balls; place 2 inches apart on ungreased baking sheets. Flatten each ball in a crisscross pattern with a fork dipped in flour. Bake at 450° for 8 to 10 minutes or until lightly browned. Cool on wire racks. Yield: 2½ dozen.

Mexicali Snack Mix

PREP: **7** MINUTES; BAKE: **20** MINUTES

1½ cups bite-size crispy wheat
    cereal squares
1½ cups roasted salted peanuts
1 cup salted sunflower kernels
1 cup Cornnuts

¼ cup butter or margarine,
    melted
2 teaspoons chili powder
¼ teaspoon ground cumin
¼ teaspoon dried crushed red
    pepper
⅛ teaspoon garlic powder

1 Combine first 4 ingredients; spread evenly in an ungreased 15- x 10- x 1-inch jellyroll pan.

2 Drizzle butter evenly over cereal mixture; stir well. Sprinkle mixture evenly with chili powder and remaining ingredients; stir well.

3 Bake, uncovered, at 350° for 20 minutes, stirring after 10 minutes. Cool completely. Store in an airtight container at room temperature. Yield: 5 cups.

To prevent Mexicali Snack Mix from becoming chewy, make sure it is completely cool before sealing it in an airtight container.

Cheesy Olive Appetizers

PREP: **10** MINUTES; BROIL: **2** MINUTES

1 (4-ounce) can chopped ripe
    olives, drained
¾ cup (3 ounces) shredded
    Cheddar cheese
¼ cup thinly sliced green onions
¼ cup mayonnaise
¼ teaspoon curry powder

6 English muffins, halved and
    toasted

1 Combine first 5 ingredients, stirring until blended.

2 Spread olive mixture evenly over cut sides of muffin halves. Place muffin halves on an ungreased baking sheet. Broil 5½ inches from heat (with electric oven door partially opened) 2 minutes or until cheese melts. Cut each muffin half into quarters, and serve immediately. Yield: 4 dozen.

Easy Nachos

PREP: 25 MINUTES; BAKE: 5 MINUTES

1 (14-ounce) package tortilla
   chips
1 (16-ounce) can refried beans
½ cup chopped green onions
1 cup (4 ounces) shredded
   Cheddar cheese
1 (12-ounce) jar pickled jalapeño
   pepper slices

1 Place 3 dozen chips on a large ungreased baking sheet. Spread 2 teaspoons refried beans on each chip; sprinkle with green onions and cheese. Top each chip with a pepper slice. Reserve remaining chips and pepper slices for other uses.

2 Bake at 350° for 5 minutes. Serve immediately. Yield: 3 dozen.

Sausage Hot Puffs

PREP: 30 MINUTES; BAKE: 12 MINUTES

FYI

Thaw frozen puff pastry in the refrigerator for 8 hours or at room temperature for 20 minutes. Refrigerate thawed puff pastry until you're ready to use it—you'll find it easier to work with dough that's chilled.

1 (17¼-ounce) package frozen
   puff pastry, thawed
Cornmeal

1 pound hot smoked link sausage,
   cut into ½-inch slices
½ cup pickled jalapeño pepper
   slices, drained

1 Roll 1 puff pastry sheet into a 15- x 12-inch rectangle on a surface lightly sprinkled with cornmeal. Cut into 3-inch squares.

2 Place 1 sausage slice and 1 pepper slice in center of each square. Fold corners to center, slightly overlapping edges. Place packets, seam side down, on greased baking sheets sprinkled with cornmeal.

3 Bake at 400° for 12 to 15 minutes or until puffed and golden. Serve immediately. Yield: 40 appetizers.

Note: Freeze unbaked puffs up to 3 months, if desired. Thaw at room temperature, and bake according to above directions.

Oriental Chicken Appetizers

Oriental Chicken Appetizers

PREP: 18 MINUTES; MARINATE: 1 HOUR; BROIL: 6 MINUTES

4 skinned and boned chicken
    breast halves, each cut into
    4 strips
1/2 cup soy sauce
2 tablespoons dark sesame oil
1 teaspoon ground ginger
3 green onions, sliced
2 cloves garlic, minced

2 tablespoons sesame seeds,
    toasted

Garnish: green onion fans
Sweet-and-sour sauce

1 Combine first 6 ingredients in a heavy-duty, zip-top plastic bag. Seal bag; marinate in refrigerator 1 hour.

2 Remove chicken from marinade; discard marinade. Weave 1 strip onto each of 16 wooden skewers; sprinkle with sesame seeds. Place on a greased rack of a broiler pan; broil 5½ inches from heat (with electric oven door partially opened) 3 minutes. Turn and broil 3 minutes or until done.

3 Arrange skewers on a serving platter; garnish, if desired. Serve appetizers with sweet-and-sour sauce. Yield: 16 appetizers.

Oklahoma Sunrise

PREP: 9 MINUTES; CHILL: 1 HOUR

FYI

Stir gently when adding champagne to a beverage. Doing so helps retain the effervescent bubbles for which champagne is famous.

1 (12-ounce) can frozen orange
  juice concentrate, thawed
  and undiluted
1 (11.5-ounce) can apricot nectar,
  chilled
3 cups water

1½ pints strawberry or raspberry
  sorbet, softened
1 (750-milliliter) bottle
  champagne, chilled
3 cups crushed ice
Garnish: whole strawberries

1 Combine first 3 ingredients in a large container; cover and chill at least 1 hour.

2 Spoon sorbet into a punch bowl; pour chilled orange juice mixture over sorbet. Add champagne and ice; stir gently to blend. Ladle into stemmed glasses, and garnish, if desired. Yield: 1 gallon.

Lemon-Lime Margaritas

PREP: 12 MINUTES

2 tablespoons fresh lime juice
Margarita salt

1 cup tequila
½ cup powdered sugar
¼ cup Triple Sec
¼ cup fresh lime juice
¼ cup fresh lemon juice
Crushed ice
Garnishes: lemon and lime rind
  strips

1 Place 2 tablespoons lime juice and margarita salt in separate saucers. Dip rims of 6 widemouthed glasses into lime juice and then into salt.

2 Combine tequila and next 4 ingredients in container of an electric blender; add enough ice to make mixture measure 4 cups. Cover and process until smooth and frothy. Pour mixture into prepared glasses, and serve immediately. Garnish, if desired. Yield: 4 cups.

Vodka Slush

PREP: 15 MINUTES; FREEZE: 2 HOURS

1 (12-ounce) can frozen lemonade
    concentrate, thawed and
    undiluted
1 (12-ounce) can frozen limeade
    concentrate, thawed and
    undiluted
1 (6-ounce) can frozen orange
    juice concentrate, thawed
    and undiluted
3½ cups water
2 cups vodka
½ cup sugar

1 (2-liter) bottle lemon-lime
    carbonated beverage, chilled

1 Combine first 6 ingredients in a large plastic container; cover and freeze 2 hours or until firm.

2 Remove mixture from freezer; let stand 10 minutes. Spoon ¾ cup slush mixture into each glass. Add ¾ cup carbonated beverage to each glass. Stir gently, and serve immediately. Yield: 13 servings.

Spirited Hot Mocha

PREP: 6 MINUTES; MICROWAVE: 6 MINUTES

2 cups milk
2 tablespoons sugar
1 tablespoon instant coffee
    granules
2 tablespoons chocolate syrup
¼ cup brandy (optional)
Sweetened whipped cream
    (optional)

1 Pour milk into a 4-cup glass measure; microwave at HIGH 6 minutes or until hot. Stir in sugar, coffee granules, chocolate syrup, and, if desired, brandy. Pour into mugs, and top with whipped cream, if desired. Yield: 2 cups.

Fruited Mint Tea

Fruited Mint Tea

PREP: 18 MINUTES

FYI

Always start with fresh, cold water when brewing tea. Hot tap water has little oxygen, so you'll get flat tea if you brew with it.

3 cups boiling water
12 fresh mint sprigs
4 regular-size tea bags

1 cup sugar
5 cups cold water
1 cup orange juice
¼ cup lemon juice
**Garnishes: fresh mint sprigs,
    fresh orange wedges**

1 Pour boiling water over 12 mint sprigs and tea bags. Cover and let stand 5 minutes.

2 Remove and discard mint sprigs and tea bags, squeezing tea bags gently. Add sugar, stirring until dissolved. Stir in cold water, orange juice, and lemon juice. Serve over ice. Garnish, if desired. Yield: about 2½ quarts.

Minted Apple Cooler

PREP: 10 MINUTES; COOK: 5 MINUTES; CHILL: 15 MINUTES

1½ cups water
¾ cup sugar
½ cup coarsely chopped fresh
    mint

4 cups apple juice
1 cup orange juice
½ cup lemon juice
Garnish: fresh mint sprigs

1 Combine first 3 ingredients in a small saucepan; bring to a boil. Reduce heat, and simmer, uncovered, 5 minutes. Cover and chill 15 minutes.

2 Pour mint mixture through a wire-mesh strainer into a large pitcher, discarding mint. Stir in juices. Serve over ice, and garnish, if desired. Yield: 7¼ cups.

Sparkling Sipper

PREP: 5 MINUTES

⅓ cup sugar
⅓ cup lemon juice
⅓ cup orange juice
1 (25.4-ounce) bottle sparkling
    red grape juice, chilled

1 Combine first 3 ingredients in a large pitcher, stirring until sugar dissolves. Add grape juice, stirring gently to blend. Serve over crushed ice. Yield: 4 cups.

Hot Buttered Lemonade

PREP: 8 MINUTES

3 cups water
½ cup sugar
2 tablespoons butter or margarine
1 teaspoon grated lemon rind

½ cup fresh lemon juice (about
    3 lemons)
Garnish: thin lemon slices

1 Combine first 4 ingredients in a saucepan; bring to a boil, stirring until sugar dissolves.

2 Stir in lemon juice. Serve warm. Garnish, if desired. Yield: 4 cups.

Looking for entrées that can be on the table in a flash? You've come to the right place. These quick main dishes include something for everyone—from **GRILLED FLORIDA TUNA** to **ENCHILADA CASSEROLE** to

Entrées

CHICKEN-PECAN FETTUCCINE. You can even turn to the recipes in this chapter for those special occasions when you want to serve an impressive entrée without cooking all day. And most of the recipes rely on ingredients you probably already have on hand.

Oriental Turkey Sauté (page 123)

Baked Grouper for Two

PREP: 5 MINUTES; COOK: 23 MINUTES

2 (8-ounce) grouper fillets
2 tablespoons butter or
    margarine, melted
2 tablespoons lemon juice
1 green onion, sliced
1 tablespoon chopped fresh
    parsley
¼ teaspoon garlic salt
⅛ teaspoon lemon-pepper
    seasoning
Paprika

Garnish: lemon wedges

1 Place fish in a lightly greased 9-inch square pan. Drizzle butter and lemon juice over fish; sprinkle with green onion and next 4 ingredients.

2 Bake at 350° for 20 minutes. Broil 5½ inches from heat (with electric oven door partially opened) 3 to 5 minutes or until fish flakes easily when tested with a fork.

3 Transfer fish to a serving platter; drizzle with butter mixture from pan. Garnish, if desired. Yield: 2 servings.

Salmon Steaks with Tarragon-Chive Butter

PREP: 8 MINUTES; GRILL: 16 MINUTES

F·Y·I

Spray the grill rack with vegetable cooking spray to keep the fish from sticking as it cooks.

¼ cup butter or margarine,
    softened
1 tablespoon chopped fresh
    tarragon
1 tablespoon chopped fresh chives
1 tablespoon Dijon mustard
1½ teaspoons chopped fresh
    parsley
⅛ teaspoon freshly ground
    pepper
1 shallot, minced

4 (1½-inch-thick) salmon steaks

1 Combine first 7 ingredients.

2 Brush fish with half of butter mixture. Grill fish, uncovered, over medium-hot coals (350° to 400°) 8 minutes on each side or until fish flakes easily when tested with a fork, brushing frequently with remaining butter mixture. Yield: 4 servings.

Pan-Fried Fish Fillets

PREP: 9 MINUTES; COOK: 10 MINUTES

¼ cup all-purpose flour
¼ teaspoon salt
¼ teaspoon ground white pepper
2 (6-ounce) red snapper or
    orange roughy fillets

1 large egg, lightly beaten
1 tablespoon milk
¼ cup Italian-seasoned
    breadcrumbs

3 tablespoons butter or
    margarine

1 Combine first 3 ingredients in a small shallow pan or dish; dredge fish in flour mixture.

2 Combine egg and milk in a small bowl; dip fish in egg mixture, and dredge in breadcrumbs.

3 Melt butter in a heavy skillet over medium heat; add fish, and cook 5 minutes on each side or until fish flakes easily when tested with a fork. Yield: 2 servings.

Glazed Swordfish Steaks

PREP: 5 MINUTES; COOK: 20 MINUTES

¼ cup firmly packed dark brown
    sugar
¼ cup butter or margarine
2 tablespoons soy sauce
2 tablespoons dry sherry

4 (1¼-inch-thick) swordfish
    steaks

Garnish: fresh watercress sprigs

1 Combine first 4 ingredients in a small saucepan; cook over low heat until sugar dissolves, stirring occasionally. Divide mixture in half.

2 Place fish on a lightly greased rack of a foil-lined broiler pan; brush fish with half of sugar mixture. Broil 5½ inches from heat (with electric oven door partially opened) 8 minutes on each side or until fish flakes easily when tested with a fork.

3 Brush fish with remaining half of sugar mixture. Transfer fish to a serving platter, and garnish, if desired. Yield: 4 servings.

Tuna Steaks with Tarragon Butter

PREP: 6 MINUTES; COOK: 10 MINUTES

*F**Y**I*

Prepare the tarragon butter several hours in advance, and chill. The tarragon flavor will intensify as the butter chills.

2 tablespoons butter or
   margarine, softened
½ teaspoon minced fresh
   tarragon
¼ teaspoon lemon juice

2 (1-inch-thick) tuna steaks
¼ teaspoon salt
¼ teaspoon freshly ground
   pepper
1 tablespoon olive oil
Garnish: fresh tarragon sprigs

1 Combine first 3 ingredients in a small bowl; set aside.

2 Sprinkle fish with salt and pepper. Cook fish in hot oil in a large nonstick skillet over medium heat 5 minutes on each side or until fish flakes easily when tested with a fork. Serve with butter mixture. Garnish, if desired. Yield: 2 servings.

Tuna Steaks with Tarragon Butter (above), Sautéed Sweet Peppers (page 157)

Grilled Florida Tuna

PREP: 3 MINUTES; GRILL: 6 MINUTES

½ cup mayonnaise
1 tablespoon lime juice
½ teaspoon ground red pepper
½ teaspoon ground cumin
1 clove garlic, crushed

4 (¾-inch-thick) tuna steaks

1 Combine first 5 ingredients.

2 Brush mayonnaise mixture on both sides of fish. Grill fish, covered, over medium coals (300° to 350°) 3 to 4 minutes on each side or until fish flakes easily when tested with a fork. Yield: 4 servings.

Crabmeat Ravigote

PREP: 15 MINUTES; COOK: 7 MINUTES

½ cup finely chopped green
    pepper
⅓ cup sliced green onions
1 (4-ounce) can sliced
    mushrooms, drained
⅓ cup butter or margarine,
    melted

⅓ cup dry sherry
1 teaspoon dried parsley flakes
½ teaspoon garlic salt
½ teaspoon celery seeds
¼ teaspoon ground white pepper
1 (2-ounce) jar diced pimiento,
    drained
1 pound fresh lump crabmeat,
    drained
½ cup soft breadcrumbs, divided

1 Cook first 3 ingredients in butter in a large skillet over medium-high heat, stirring constantly, until vegetables are tender.

2 Stir sherry and next 5 ingredients into vegetable mixture. Add crabmeat and ¼ cup breadcrumbs; stir gently.

3 Spoon crabmeat mixture into 4 lightly greased (8-ounce) ramekins. Sprinkle remaining ¼ cup breadcrumbs evenly over servings.

4 Broil 5½ inches from heat (with electric oven door partially opened) 1 minute or until lightly browned. Yield: 4 servings.

Lemon-Garlic Broiled Shrimp

PREP: 5 MINUTES; COOK: 10 MINUTES

2 cloves garlic, minced
1 cup butter or margarine,
  melted
¼ cup lemon juice
½ teaspoon salt
¼ teaspoon pepper

1 pound peeled and deveined
  large fresh shrimp
  (1⅓ pounds unpeeled)

1 Cook garlic in butter in a small saucepan over medium heat, stirring constantly, until tender. Remove from heat; stir in lemon juice, salt, and pepper.

2 Arrange shrimp in a single layer in a shallow pan; pour butter mixture over shrimp. Broil 5½ inches from heat (with electric oven door partially opened) 5 minutes or until shrimp turn pink, basting once with butter mixture. Serve with crusty French bread. Yield: 4 servings.

Shrimp and Pasta

PREP: 15 MINUTES; COOK: 12 MINUTES

8 ounces spaghetti, uncooked
1 tablespoon Old Bay seasoning

1 cup broccoli flowerets
1 clove garlic, minced
3 tablespoons olive oil
1 bunch green onions, chopped
1 pound peeled and deveined
  medium-size fresh shrimp
  (1⅓ pounds unpeeled)
1 (4-ounce) can sliced
  mushrooms, drained
½ (8-ounce) can sliced water
  chestnuts, drained

½ cup sour cream
Grated Parmesan cheese

1 Cook spaghetti according to package directions, omitting salt and adding Old Bay seasoning; drain.

2 While spaghetti cooks, cook broccoli and garlic in hot oil in a skillet over medium-high heat, stirring constantly, 3 minutes. Add green onions; cook 1 minute. Add shrimp; cook, stirring constantly, 5 minutes or until shrimp turn pink. Stir in mushrooms and water chestnuts.

3 Reduce heat to low; stir in sour cream. Cook, stirring constantly, until thoroughly heated. (Do not boil.) Serve shrimp mixture over spaghetti; sprinkle with Parmesan cheese. Yield: 4 servings.

Quick Scampi

Quick Scampi

PREP: 5 MINUTES; COOK: 10 MINUTES

1½ tablespoons sliced green
    onions
¾ teaspoon grated lemon rind
1½ tablespoons fresh lemon juice
¼ teaspoon salt
2 large cloves garlic, minced
⅓ cup butter or margarine,
    melted

¾ pound peeled and deveined
    large fresh shrimp (1 pound
    unpeeled)

2 tablespoons minced fresh
    parsley
¼ teaspoon hot sauce
Hot cooked angel hair pasta
Garnishes: lemon slices, fresh
    parsley sprigs

1 Cook first 5 ingredients in butter in a large skillet over medium-high heat, stirring constantly, until mixture is bubbly.

2 Reduce heat to medium; add shrimp to onion mixture, and cook, stirring constantly, 5 minutes or until shrimp turn pink.

3 Add minced parsley and hot sauce to shrimp mixture; toss gently. Serve over hot cooked pasta. Garnish, if desired. Yield: 2 servings.

FYI

Cook shrimp just until they appear opaque and turn pink. Overcooked shrimp will be tough and rubbery.

Beef with Tomatoes and Artichokes

PREP: 20 MINUTES; MARINATE: 8 HOURS; GRILL: 15 MINUTES

2 (1½-inch-thick) beef tenderloin
    steaks (about 1 pound)
Italian Marinade

½ cup oil-packed dried tomatoes
1½ tablespoons finely chopped
    green onions
1 clove garlic, minced
1 (14-ounce) can artichoke hearts,
    drained and quartered
¼ teaspoon dried basil

1 Place steaks in a heavy-duty, zip-top plastic bag, and add Italian Marinade. Seal bag, and marinate in refrigerator 8 hours, turning bag occasionally.

2 Drain tomatoes, reserving 1 table-spoon oil. Chop tomatoes. Heat reserved oil in a large skillet over medium-high heat. Add green onions and garlic; cook, stirring constantly, 2 minutes. Add chopped tomato, artichoke, and basil; cook 5 minutes, stirring often. Set aside, and keep warm.

3 Remove steaks from marinade, discarding marinade. Grill, uncovered, over medium-hot coals (350° to 400°) 6 to 8 minutes on each side or to desired degree of doneness. Slice steak diagonally across grain into thin slices, and serve with warm tomato mixture. Yield: 2 servings.

Italian Marinade

1 tablespoon finely chopped onion
1 tablespoon olive oil
2 teaspoons red wine vinegar
½ teaspoon dry mustard
¼ teaspoon dried basil
¼ teaspoon dried rosemary
⅛ teaspoon salt
⅛ teaspoon pepper
1 clove garlic, minced

1 Combine all ingredients in a jar. Cover tightly, and shake vigorously. Yield: 3 tablespoons.

Beef and Broccoli

PREP: **20** MINUTES; COOK: **10** MINUTES

1 **pound boneless sirloin steak**

3 **tablespoons vegetable oil,
   divided**

3 **cups broccoli flowerets**

2 **tablespoons soy sauce**
2 **teaspoons cornstarch**
⅔ **cup chicken broth**
2 **tablespoons sherry (optional)**
½ **teaspoon sugar**
Hot cooked rice

1 Trim excess fat from steak. Slice steak diagonally across grain into thin strips.

2 Pour 1 tablespoon oil around top of preheated wok or large skillet, coating sides; heat at medium-high (375°) for 2 minutes. Add steak, and stir-fry 2 to 3 minutes or until no longer pink. Remove steak from wok; set aside. Discard liquid in wok, and wipe wok with paper towels.

3 Pour remaining 2 tablespoons oil around top of wok, coating sides; heat at medium-high for 2 minutes. Add broccoli, and stir-fry 2 to 3 minutes or until crisp-tender. Remove broccoli from wok, and set aside.

4 Combine soy sauce and cornstarch in a small bowl; add broth, sherry, if desired, and sugar. Add soy sauce mixture to wok; cook over medium heat until thickened and bubbly. Add steak and broccoli to wok, and stir-fry 2 minutes. Serve over rice. Yield: 4 servings.

To keep preparation time short, purchase bags of ready-to-use broccoli flowerets in the produce section of your supermarket.

Pepper Steak Stir-Fry

PREP: 18 MINUTES; COOK: 12 MINUTES

½ cup canned beef broth,
    undiluted
¼ cup water
¼ cup soy sauce
1 tablespoon cornstarch

1¼ pounds boneless sirloin steak

¼ cup vegetable oil
1 clove garlic, minced
1 teaspoon ground ginger
½ teaspoon salt
½ teaspoon pepper

1 large green pepper, seeded and
    cut into strips
1 large sweet red pepper, seeded
    and cut into strips
1 large onion, thinly sliced
1 (8-ounce) can sliced water
    chestnuts, drained
4 green onions, cut into 1-inch
    pieces
Hot cooked rice

1 Combine first 4 ingredients in a small bowl; set aside.

2 Trim excess fat from steak. Slice steak diagonally across grain into thin strips.

3 Pour oil around top of preheated wok or skillet, coating sides; heat at medium-high (375°) 2 minutes. Add garlic and next 3 ingredients; stir-fry 1 minute. Add steak to wok, and stir-fry 2 minutes or until no longer pink. Remove steak from wok, and drain on paper towels; set aside.

4 Add pepper strips and sliced onion to wok; stir-fry 5 minutes or until crisp-tender. Add steak, water chestnuts, green onions, and beef broth mixture; stir-fry 2 minutes or until mixture is thickened. Serve beef mixture over rice. Yield: 4 servings.

Enchilada Casserole

Enchilada Casserole

PREP: 5 MINUTES; COOK: 25 MINUTES

2 pounds ground chuck
1 medium onion, chopped

2 (8-ounce) cans tomato sauce
1 (11-ounce) can Mexicorn, drained
1 (10-ounce) can enchilada sauce
1 teaspoon chili powder
½ teaspoon dried oregano
½ teaspoon pepper
¼ teaspoon salt

1 (6½-ounce) package corn tortillas, divided
2 cups (8 ounces) shredded Cheddar cheese, divided
Garnish: green chile peppers

1 Cook beef and onion in a large skillet until beef is browned, stirring until it crumbles; drain.

2 Stir tomato sauce and next 6 ingredients into meat mixture; bring to a boil. Reduce heat to medium, and cook, uncovered, 5 minutes, stirring occasionally.

3 Place half of tortillas in bottom of a greased 13- x 9- x 2-inch baking dish. Spoon half of beef mixture over tortillas; sprinkle with 1 cup cheese. Repeat layers with remaining tortillas and beef mixture. Bake at 375° for 10 minutes. Sprinkle with remaining cheese; bake 5 additional minutes or until cheese melts. Garnish, if desired. Yield: 8 servings.

Hamburger Stroganoff

PREP: 5 MINUTES; COOK: 25 MINUTES

1 pound ground chuck
4 slices bacon, chopped
1 small onion, chopped

1 (10¾-ounce) can cream of
  mushroom soup, undiluted
½ teaspoon salt
¼ teaspoon paprika
1 (8-ounce) carton sour cream
Hot cooked noodles

1 Cook first 3 ingredients in a large skillet over medium-high heat until beef is browned and onion is tender, stirring until beef crumbles; drain.

2 Stir soup, salt, and paprika into beef mixture. Cook, uncovered, over medium heat 15 minutes, stirring occasionally. Stir in sour cream; cook until thoroughly heated. (Do not boil.) Serve beef mixture over noodles. Yield: 4 servings.

Lemon Veal with Artichoke Hearts

PREP: 10 MINUTES; COOK: 10 MINUTES

⅓ cup all-purpose flour
¼ teaspoon salt
1 pound veal cutlets

2 tablespoons butter or
  margarine

1 cup chicken broth
¼ cup lemon juice
¼ cup dry vermouth
2 tablespoons Worcestershire
  sauce
1 teaspoon dried marjoram
½ teaspoon minced garlic
1 bay leaf

1 (14-ounce) can artichoke hearts,
  drained
Hot cooked linguine
Garnishes: lemon slices, fresh
  parsley sprigs

1 Combine flour and salt in a large heavy-duty, zip-top plastic bag. Seal bag; shake well. Add veal; shake until veal is coated.

2 Melt butter in a large skillet over medium-high heat. Add veal, and cook 1 to 2 minutes on each side or until done. Remove veal from skillet, and drain on paper towels.

3 Add chicken broth and next 6 ingredients to skillet; bring to a boil, stirring often.

4 Add veal and artichoke hearts to skillet; cover, reduce heat, and simmer 5 minutes. Remove and discard bay leaf. Serve over pasta; garnish, if desired. Yield: 4 servings.

Veal Piccata

PREP: 6 MINUTES; COOK: 6 MINUTES

⅓ cup all-purpose flour
¾ teaspoon salt
¼ teaspoon pepper
⅛ teaspoon garlic powder
½ pound veal cutlets

¼ cup butter or margarine

1 tablespoon chopped fresh
   parsley
3 tablespoons fresh lemon juice
Garnish: lemon slices

1 Combine first 4 ingredients in a large heavy-duty, zip-top plastic bag. Seal bag; shake well. Add veal; shake until veal is coated.

2 Melt butter in a large skillet over medium-high heat. Add veal, and cook 1 to 2 minutes on each side or until done. Remove veal from skillet, and drain on paper towels.

3 Add parsley and lemon juice to skillet; stir well. Return veal to skillet; cook just until thoroughly heated. Transfer veal to a serving platter or individual plates; spoon lemon mixture over veal. Garnish, if desired. Yield: 2 servings.

FYI

You can easily keep chopped parsley on hand. After snipping one or two tablespoons from a bunch of parsley, chop the remainder. Then freeze it in an airtight freezer bag up to two months.

Destin Lamb Chops

PREP: 6 MINUTES; BROIL: 12 MINUTES

1½ tablespoons Dijon mustard
1 teaspoon Worcestershire sauce
½ teaspoon dried rosemary
¼ teaspoon dried dillweed
¼ teaspoon ground ginger
⅛ teaspoon garlic powder
¼ teaspoon prepared
   horseradish

2 (¾-inch-thick) lamb sirloin
   chops
Olive oil

1 Combine first 7 ingredients in a small bowl; set aside.

2 Trim excess fat from lamb chops. Brush chops with oil; place on a lightly greased rack of a broiler pan. Broil 5½ inches from heat (with electric oven door partially opened) 5 minutes. Turn chops, and spread with half of mustard mixture; broil 5 minutes. Turn chops again, and spread with remaining half of mustard mixture; broil 2 minutes or until bubbly. Yield: 2 servings.

Teriyaki Lamb Chops

PREP: 10 MINUTES; MARINATE: 8 HOURS; GRILL: 12 MINUTES

8 (1-inch-thick) lamb loin chops
½ cup finely chopped onion
¼ cup cider vinegar
¼ cup soy sauce
2 tablespoons honey
2 teaspoons ground ginger
¼ teaspoon dry mustard
¼ teaspoon pepper
2 cloves garlic, sliced

1 Trim excess fat from lamb chops; place in a heavy-duty, zip-top plastic bag. Combine onion and remaining ingredients; pour over chops. Seal bag, and marinate in refrigerator 8 hours, turning bag occasionally.

2 Remove chops from marinade. Place marinade in a small saucepan; bring to a boil. Remove from heat, and set aside.

3 Grill chops, covered, over medium coals (300° to 350°) 6 minutes on each side or to desired degree of doneness, basting frequently with marinade. Yield: 4 servings.

Pork Medaillons with Chutney Sauce

PREP: 10 MINUTES; COOK: 15 MINUTES

Pork tenderloins come packaged in vacuum-sealed plastic bags. You can slice the tenderloins for this recipe easily by first freezing them about 30 minutes.

1 tablespoon vegetable oil, divided
2 (¾-pound) pork tenderloins, cut into thin slices
1 clove garlic, minced and divided
⅛ teaspoon salt
⅛ teaspoon pepper

½ cup chutney
2 tablespoons grated orange rind
¼ cup fresh orange juice

1 Heat 1½ teaspoons oil in a large skillet over medium-high heat; cook half each of pork and garlic in hot oil 6 minutes or until pork is done. Transfer to a serving platter, and keep warm. Repeat procedure with remaining oil, pork, and garlic. Sprinkle with salt and pepper.

2 Combine chutney, orange rind, and juice in a small saucepan; cook over medium heat until thoroughly heated, stirring often. Serve chutney sauce with pork. Yield: 6 servings.

Savory Pork Chops

PREP: 8 MINUTES; COOK: 30 MINUTES

4 (½-inch-thick) center-cut pork
    chops
½ teaspoon salt
¼ teaspoon pepper
2 tablespoons butter or
    margarine, melted
1 large Granny Smith apple,
    cored and sliced
¼ cup golden raisins
1 teaspoon grated lemon rind
    (optional)
½ cup apple juice

1 Sprinkle pork chops with salt and pepper. Brown chops in butter in a large skillet over medium-high heat. Top with apple slices, raisins, and, if desired, lemon rind. Add apple juice; cover, reduce heat, and simmer 30 minutes or until chops are tender. Yield: 4 servings.

Pork Chops Parmigiana

PREP: 9 MINUTES; BAKE: 30 MINUTES

1 large egg, lightly beaten
1 tablespoon water
⅓ cup Italian-seasoned
    breadcrumbs
2 tablespoons grated Parmesan
    cheese

4 (½-inch-thick) pork loin chops
2 tablespoons vegetable oil
1 cup spaghetti sauce

½ cup (2 ounces) shredded
    mozzarella cheese

1 Combine egg and water in a small shallow dish. Combine breadcrumbs and Parmesan cheese in a small shallow dish.

2 Dip chops in egg mixture, and dredge in breadcrumb mixture. Brown chops in hot oil in a large skillet over medium heat. Arrange chops in a lightly greased 8-inch square baking dish, and top with spaghetti sauce.

3 Bake at 350° for 25 minutes. Sprinkle with mozzarella cheese; bake 5 additional minutes or until cheese melts. Yield: 4 servings.

Cranberry Broiled Ham

PREP: 5 MINUTES; BROIL: 25 MINUTES

1 (1-inch-thick) slice fully cooked
   ham (about 2 pounds)

½ (16-ounce) can jellied
   cranberry sauce
2½ tablespoons steak sauce
1½ teaspoons brown sugar
1½ teaspoons vegetable oil
1 teaspoon prepared mustard

1 Trim excess fat from ham. Place ham in a lightly greased 13- x 9- x 2-inch pan; broil 5½ inches from heat (with electric oven door partially opened) 15 minutes.

2 Combine cranberry sauce and remaining ingredients. Turn ham, and spread cranberry sauce mixture on top; broil 10 additional minutes. Yield: 6 servings.

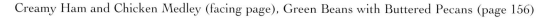

Creamy Ham and Chicken Medley (facing page), Green Beans with Buttered Pecans (page 156)

Creamy Ham and Chicken Medley

PREP: 10 MINUTES; COOK: 25 MINUTES

2 (10-ounce) packages frozen
    puff pastry shells

1 tablespoon butter or margarine
½ cup sliced fresh mushrooms

⅓ cup butter or margarine
⅓ cup all-purpose flour
2½ cups milk
1 cup whipping cream
¾ cup freshly grated Parmesan
    cheese
½ teaspoon salt
¼ teaspoon freshly ground black
    pepper
¼ teaspoon ground nutmeg
Dash of ground red pepper
2 cups chopped cooked ham
2 cups chopped cooked chicken

Paprika

1 Bake pastry shells according to package directions.

2 While pastry shells bake, melt 1 tablespoon butter in a large saucepan over medium-high heat; add mushrooms, and cook, stirring constantly, until tender. Remove mushrooms from pan, and set aside.

3 Melt ⅓ cup butter in pan over medium heat; add flour, stirring until smooth. Cook, stirring constantly, 1 minute. Gradually add milk; cook, stirring constantly, until mixture is thickened and bubbly. Stir in whipping cream and next 5 ingredients; cook, stirring constantly, until cheese melts and mixture is smooth. Stir in mushrooms, ham, and chicken; cook until thoroughly heated, stirring often.

4 To serve, spoon mixture into baked pastry shells, and sprinkle with paprika. Yield: 12 servings.

Note: Serve mixture over hot cooked angel hair pasta, and sprinkle with freshly grated Parmesan cheese, if desired.

FYI

Grating Parmesan cheese? Cleanup is a breeze when you lightly brush the grater with oil or spray it with vegetable cooking spray before grating.

Italian Sausage and Peppers

PREP: 5 MINUTES; COOK: 25 MINUTES

1 pound mild Italian link sausage, cut into 1-inch pieces

4 medium-size green peppers, seeded and cut into 1-inch pieces
1 large onion, cut into eighths
2 (16-ounce) jars marinara sauce

Hot cooked spaghetti
Grated Romano cheese
Chopped fresh parsley

1 Brown sausage in a Dutch oven over medium heat. Remove sausage with a slotted spoon, reserving drippings in Dutch oven; set aside.

2 Cook green pepper and onion in drippings 5 to 6 minutes or until tender; add sausage and marinara sauce. Reduce heat, and simmer, uncovered, 10 minutes, stirring occasionally.

3 Spoon sausage mixture over pasta; sprinkle with Romano cheese and parsley. Yield: 8 servings.

Lemon-Pepper Chicken

PREP: 10 MINUTES; COOK: 9 MINUTES

4 skinned and boned chicken breast halves

¼ cup all-purpose flour
½ teaspoon lemon-pepper seasoning
¼ teaspoon salt

¼ cup butter or margarine, melted
1 tablespoon lemon juice

1 Place chicken between 2 sheets of heavy-duty plastic wrap; flatten to ¼-inch thickness using a meat mallet or rolling pin.

2 Combine flour, lemon-pepper seasoning, and salt; dredge chicken lightly in flour mixture.

3 Cook chicken in butter in a large skillet over medium heat 3 minutes on each side or until golden. Add lemon juice, and cook 3 additional minutes. Yield: 4 servings.

Chicken and Mushrooms Marsala

PREP: 10 MINUTES; COOK: 25 MINUTES

½ cup all-purpose flour
½ teaspoon salt
½ teaspoon freshly ground
    pepper
1½ pounds skinned and boned
    chicken breast halves

¼ cup olive oil

½ pound fresh mushrooms, sliced

⅔ cup chopped green onions
6 medium tomatoes, seeded and
    chopped
½ teaspoon salt
½ teaspoon dried basil
1½ cups Marsala

Hot cooked angel hair pasta
    (optional)
½ cup freshly grated Parmesan
    cheese
¼ cup chopped fresh parsley
Garnish: fresh basil sprigs

1 Combine first 3 ingredients in a large heavy-duty, zip-top plastic bag. Add chicken to flour mixture, a few pieces at a time; seal bag, and shake until chicken is well coated.

2 Heat oil in a large skillet over medium heat. Add chicken, and cook 5 minutes on each side or until done; remove chicken, and drain on paper towels.

3 Add mushrooms to skillet; cook over medium-high heat, stirring constantly, until tender. Remove mushrooms from skillet, and set aside; reserve pan drippings in skillet.

4 Add green onions to drippings; cook, stirring constantly, until tender. Stir in tomato, salt, and basil; cook 4 to 5 minutes or until most of liquid evaporates. Add Marsala, and simmer, uncovered, 8 minutes or until thickened.

5 Return chicken and mushrooms to skillet, and cook until thoroughly heated. Serve with hot cooked pasta, if desired. Sprinkle with Parmesan cheese and parsley. Garnish, if desired. Yield: 6 servings.

For variation, substitute veal cutlets for the chicken and hot cooked rice for the angel hair pasta in this recipe.

Chicken-Pecan Fettuccine

PREP: 7 MINUTES; COOK: 18 MINUTES

FYI

Cut chicken quickly into ³/₄-inch pieces with kitchen shears.

10 ounces fettuccine, uncooked

¼ cup butter or margarine
1¼ pounds skinned and boned chicken breast halves, cut into ³/₄-inch pieces

3 cups sliced fresh mushrooms
1 cup sliced green onions
½ teaspoon salt
¼ teaspoon freshly ground pepper
1 clove garlic, crushed

¾ cup half-and-half
½ cup butter or margarine, melted
¼ cup chopped fresh parsley
¼ teaspoon salt
¼ teaspoon garlic powder
¼ teaspoon pepper
½ cup freshly grated Parmesan cheese
1 cup coarsely chopped pecans, toasted

1 Cook fettuccine according to package directions, omitting salt. Drain well.

2 While fettuccine cooks, melt ¼ cup butter in a large skillet over medium heat; add chicken, and cook until browned on all sides. Remove chicken from skillet, and set aside, reserving drippings in skillet.

3 Add mushrooms and next 4 ingredients to drippings; cook, stirring constantly, until vegetables are tender. Add chicken; cook 15 minutes or until chicken is done, stirring occasionally.

4 Combine half-and-half and next 5 ingredients; stir into fettuccine. Add cheese; toss well. Add chicken mixture; toss well. Spoon mixture into a serving bowl; sprinkle with pecans. Serve immediately. Yield: 6 servings.

Chicken-Pecan Fettuccine (facing page)

Parmesan Baked Chicken

PREP: 10 MINUTES; BAKE: 25 MINUTES

½ cup fine, dry breadcrumbs
¼ cup grated Parmesan cheese
½ teaspoon dried basil
½ teaspoon dried thyme
¼ teaspoon salt

4 skinned and boned chicken breast halves
¼ cup butter or margarine, melted

1 Combine first 5 ingredients in a heavy-duty, zip-top plastic bag; seal bag, and shake well.

2 Dip chicken in butter. Add 1 piece of chicken at a time to breadcrumb mixture; seal bag, and shake until well coated. Place chicken on a greased baking sheet. Bake at 400° for 25 to 30 minutes or until done. Yield: 4 servings.

FYI

Using a heavy-duty zip-top plastic bag for dredging makes cleanup quick and easy.

Easy Chicken à la King

PREP: **9** MINUTES; COOK: **25** MINUTES

2 frozen puff pastry shells

1 cup chopped cooked chicken
¼ cup milk
½ teaspoon salt
⅛ teaspoon pepper
1 (10¾-ounce) can cream of
    chicken soup, undiluted
1 (4-ounce) can sliced
    mushrooms, drained
1 (2-ounce) jar diced pimiento,
    drained

1 Bake pastry shells according to package directions.

2 While pastry shells bake, combine chicken and remaining ingredients in a medium saucepan; cook over low heat 10 minutes or until thoroughly heated, stirring often. Serve chicken mixture over baked pastry shells. Yield: 2 servings.

Chicken and Bean Tacos (facing page)

Chicken and Bean Tacos

PREP: 15 MINUTES; COOK: 20 MINUTES

1 (15-ounce) can refried beans

8 (6-inch) flour tortillas
8 taco shells

2/3 cup chopped onion
1/3 cup chopped green pepper
2 tablespoons vegetable oil
2 cups shredded cooked chicken
1 (16-ounce) jar taco sauce
1½ teaspoons chili powder
1 teaspoon sugar

2 cups shredded iceberg lettuce
1 cup chopped tomato
1 cup (4 ounces) shredded
    Cheddar cheese

1 Cook refried beans in a small saucepan over medium-low heat until thoroughly heated, stirring occasionally; set aside, and keep warm.

2 Heat tortillas and taco shells according to package directions; set aside, and keep warm.

3 Cook onion and green pepper in hot oil in a heavy saucepan over medium heat, stirring constantly, until tender. Stir in chicken and next 3 ingredients; cook until thoroughly heated.

4 For each taco, spread about 2 tablespoons refried beans over a flour tortilla to within ½ inch of edge. Place a taco shell in center of tortilla, and press tortilla up and onto sides of taco shell. Fill taco shell with about ⅓ cup chicken mixture, ¼ cup shredded lettuce, 2 tablespoons tomato, and 2 tablespoons cheese. Serve immediately. Yield: 8 tacos.

Note: To save time, let everyone assemble their own tacos.

FYI

Warm the tortillas for this recipe in the microwave by stacking and wrapping them in a damp paper towel. Then microwave at HIGH for 1 minute. It's quicker than warming them in the oven.

Lime-Buttered Turkey Tenderloins

Lime-Buttered Turkey Tenderloins

PREP: 2 MINUTES; GRILL: 16 MINUTES

¼ cup butter or margarine, melted
¼ cup lime juice
2 teaspoons dry mustard
1½ teaspoons garlic salt

2 (¾-pound) turkey breast tenderloins
Garnishes: lime wedges, fresh parsley sprigs

1 Combine first 4 ingredients; divide mixture in half, and set aside.

2 Grill tenderloins, covered, over medium-hot coals (350° to 400°) 8 to 9 minutes on each side or until done, turning once and basting with half of lime juice mixture. Remove from grill, and keep warm.

3 Cook remaining half of lime juice mixture in a small saucepan over low heat until thoroughly heated. Slice tenderloins, and serve with warm lime juice mixture. Garnish, if desired. Yield: 6 servings.

Oriental Turkey Sauté

PREP: 6 MINUTES; COOK: 9 MINUTES

¼ cup water
2 tablespoons soy sauce
2 teaspoons cornstarch
1 teaspoon sugar

2 tablespoons vegetable oil
1 teaspoon grated fresh ginger
1 clove garlic, minced
1 pound boneless turkey breast,
    cut into bite-size pieces*
1 (8-ounce) can sliced water
    chestnuts, drained
1 (6-ounce) package frozen snow
    pea pods, thawed
½ small sweet red pepper, seeded
    and sliced
Hot cooked rice

1 Combine first 4 ingredients; stir well, and set aside.

2 Heat oil in a large heavy skillet over medium-high heat until hot; add ginger and garlic, and cook 1 minute or until tender. Add turkey; cook, stirring constantly, 4 to 5 minutes or until lightly browned. Add water chestnuts, snow peas, and red pepper; cook, stirring constantly, 1 minute. Add soy sauce mixture; cook 1 minute or until thickened. Serve over rice. Yield: 4 servings.

* Substitute 1 pound skinned and boned chicken breast halves, if desired.

FYI

Store fresh ginger in the freezer in a heavy-duty, zip-top plastic bag; it's easy to peel and grate while frozen.

Turkey with Tarragon-Mustard Sauce

PREP: 10 MINUTES; COOK: 6 MINUTES

½ pound turkey cutlets
1 teaspoon garlic salt
¼ teaspoon pepper
1 tablespoon olive oil

½ cup plain low-fat yogurt
2 tablespoons Dijon mustard
¼ teaspoon sugar
¼ teaspoon dried tarragon
⅛ teaspoon hot sauce

1 Sprinkle turkey with garlic salt and pepper. Cook turkey in hot oil in a large skillet over medium-high heat 2 minutes on each side or until done. Remove turkey; set aside, and keep warm.

2 Combine yogurt and remaining 4 ingredients in skillet; cook over low heat, stirring constantly, until thoroughly heated. Spoon sauce over turkey. Yield: 2 servings.

So many times, a simple salad, soup, or sandwich solves the dilemma of what to serve for lunch or supper. This chapter offers hearty selections of these classics— each substantial enough to be a meal on its own. Our

SALADS, SOUPS & SANDWICHES

highest-rated one-dish meals include **SPINACH-LAMB SALAD, CREAMY CHICKEN-VEGETABLE CHOWDER,** and **OPEN-FACED JALAPEÑO HEROES.** When time allows, team lighter versions of these specialties together for a soup-and-salad lunch or a soup-and-sandwich supper.

Smoked Sausage Sandwich (page 147), Creamy Tomato Soup (page 136)

Fruit Salad with Poppy Seed Dressing

PREP: 26 MINUTES

FYI

To keep preparation easy on the cook, purchase peeled, cored pineapple and cubed melon in the produce section of your supermarket.

1 small head romaine lettuce
2 kiwifruit, peeled and sliced
2 cups strawberries, halved
2 cups cubed fresh pineapple
2 cups cubed cantaloupe
2 cups cubed honeydew
Poppy Seed Dressing

1 Line a platter with lettuce leaves; arrange fruit on lettuce. Serve salad immediately with Poppy Seed Dressing. Yield: 6 servings.

Poppy Seed Dressing

1 cup vegetable oil
¾ cup sugar
⅓ cup white vinegar
2 tablespoons minced onion
1 teaspoon salt
½ teaspoon dry mustard

1½ teaspoons poppy seeds

1 Combine first 6 ingredients in a medium saucepan. Cook over medium heat, stirring constantly, until sugar dissolves.

2 Stir in poppy seeds. Cover and chill, if desired. Stir before serving. Yield: 1½ cups.

Strawberry-Spinach Salad

PREP: 18 MINUTES; CHILL: 30 MINUTES

¼ cup sugar
3 tablespoons lemon juice
¼ cup egg substitute
⅓ cup vegetable oil

1 (10-ounce) package fresh, trimmed spinach, torn into bite-size pieces
2 cups strawberries, sliced
1 cup pecan halves, toasted

1 Combine sugar and lemon juice in a small bowl; beat with a wire whisk until sugar dissolves. Add egg substitute; beat well. Add vegetable oil, 1 tablespoon at a time, beating until dressing is thick and creamy. Cover and chill at least 30 minutes.

2 Combine spinach, strawberries, and pecan halves in a bowl; add chilled dressing, and toss gently. Serve immediately. Yield: 8 servings.

Company Salad with Raspberry Vinaigrette

PREP: 25 MINUTES

1 head Bibb lettuce, torn into
   bite-size pieces
1 Red Delicious apple, unpeeled
   and thinly sliced
1 kiwifruit, peeled and thinly
   sliced
2 (11-ounce) cans mandarin
   oranges, drained
½ pound fresh spinach, torn into
   bite-size pieces
½ cup fresh raspberries
½ cup coarsely chopped walnuts,
   toasted

Raspberry Vinaigrette

1 Combine first 7 ingredients in a large salad bowl.

2 Drizzle Raspberry Vinaigrette over salad, and toss gently. Serve immediately. Yield: 6 servings.

Raspberry Vinaigrette
¼ cup vegetable oil
2 tablespoons raspberry-flavored
   vinegar
2 teaspoons honey
¼ teaspoon grated orange rind
⅛ teaspoon salt

1 Combine all ingredients in a jar; cover tightly, and shake vigorously. Chill, if desired. Yield: ⅓ cup.

Festive Corn Salad

PREP: 13 MINUTES

1 (11-ounce) can white whole
    kernel corn, drained and
    rinsed
1 medium-size green pepper,
    seeded and chopped
1 medium tomato, chopped
1 medium-size purple onion,
    chopped
¼ teaspoon pepper
½ cup commercial Italian salad
    dressing

Lettuce leaves

1 Combine first 6 ingredients; cover and chill, if desired.

2 Spoon corn mixture into a bowl lined with lettuce leaves. Serve with a slotted spoon. Yield: 6 servings.

French-Style Potato Salad

PREP: 15 MINUTES; COOK: 15 MINUTES; CHILL: 1 HOUR

Leaving the skins on the potatoes saves time and preserves nutrients. Just be sure to scrub the potatoes thoroughly.

1½ pounds small round red
    potatoes
3 tablespoons dry white wine

¼ cup olive oil
2 tablespoons white wine vinegar
1 to 2 tablespoons Dijon mustard
¼ teaspoon salt
¼ teaspoon ground white pepper
¼ teaspoon dried tarragon

¼ cup thinly sliced green onions
¼ cup chopped fresh parsley
Lettuce leaves

1 Cook potatoes in boiling water to cover 15 minutes or until tender; drain and cool slightly. Cut potatoes into ¼-inch-thick slices; place in a large bowl. Add wine; toss gently.

2 Combine olive oil and next 5 ingredients; pour over potato mixture.

3 Add green onions and parsley to potato mixture; toss gently. Cover and chill at least 1 hour. Spoon potato mixture onto a lettuce-lined platter or into a lettuce-lined bowl. Yield: 6 servings.

Tomato-Basil-Mozzarella Salad

Tomato-Basil-Mozzarella Salad

PREP: 9 MINUTES; CHILL: 1 HOUR

3 large ripe tomatoes, cut into
  ½-inch-thick slices (about
  1½ pounds)
12 fresh basil leaves
8 ounces mozzarella cheese, cut
  into ¼-inch-thick strips

1½ tablespoons olive oil
1½ tablespoons lemon juice
¼ teaspoon salt
¼ teaspoon freshly ground
  pepper
Garnish: fresh basil sprig

1 Arrange tomato slices on a serving platter. Top each tomato slice with a basil leaf and a cheese strip.

2 Combine oil and lemon juice; drizzle over tomato salad. Sprinkle with salt and pepper. Cover and chill at least 1 hour. Garnish, if desired. Yield: 6 servings.

Buy vine-ripened tomatoes, and store them at room temperature for maximum flavor. To speed the ripening process, place tomatoes in a paper bag.

Shrimp Salad with Sherry Vinaigrette

PREP: 20 MINUTES; COOK: 8 MINUTES; CHILL: 1 HOUR

FYI

To remove the white membrane easily when peeling an orange, soak the unpeeled orange in boiling water 5 minutes. Slice off the top to check the thickness of the peel, and cut away the rind and white membrane in a continuous strip.

6 cups water
2 pounds unpeeled medium-size
   fresh shrimp

3 tablespoons sherry vinegar
1 teaspoon sugar
1 teaspoon grated orange rind
1 clove garlic, minced
⅓ cup olive oil

2 navel oranges
1 cup pimiento-stuffed olives

5 cups torn Bibb lettuce
5 cups torn leaf lettuce
2 green onions, cut diagonally
   into 1-inch pieces

1 Bring water to a boil; add shrimp, and cook 3 to 5 minutes or until shrimp turn pink. Drain; rinse with cold water. Peel shrimp, and devein, if desired. Set aside.

2 Combine sherry vinegar and next 3 ingredients in a large bowl; gradually add olive oil, beating well with a wire whisk. Set aside.

3 Peel oranges, and cut into ½-inch-thick slices; cut slices into quarters. Add orange, olives, and shrimp to vinegar mixture; toss gently. Cover and chill at least 1 hour.

4 To serve, add lettuces and green onions to shrimp mixture, and toss gently. Yield: 6 servings.

Shrimp Salad with Sherry Vinaigrette

Spinach-Lamb Salad

PREP: 25 MINUTES; CHILL: 1 HOUR; COOK: 4 MINUTES

1 pound lean boneless lamb
1 tablespoon olive oil

½ pound fresh spinach, torn into
    bite-size pieces
1 cup crumbled feta cheese
½ cup sliced fresh mushrooms
1 medium-size green pepper,
    seeded and cut into thin
    strips

2 medium tomatoes, cut into
    wedges
Freshly ground pepper
Yogurt Dressing

1 Slice lamb diagonally across grain into thin strips. Cook lamb in hot oil in a large skillet over medium-high heat, stirring constantly, 4 to 5 minutes or until lamb is done. Drain and set aside.

2 Combine spinach and next 3 ingredients, tossing gently; arrange on a serving platter.

3 Place lamb in center of spinach mixture, and arrange tomato wedges around lamb. Sprinkle with freshly ground pepper, and serve with Yogurt Dressing. Yield: 4 servings.

Yogurt Dressing
¾ cup plain low-fat yogurt
1 tablespoon lemon juice
1 tablespoon olive oil
⅛ teaspoon salt
⅛ teaspoon ground white pepper
1 green onion, chopped
1 clove garlic, pressed

1 Combine all ingredients in a jar; cover tightly, and shake vigorously. Chill at least 1 hour. Shake well before serving. Yield: about 1 cup.

Rotini Salad

PREP: 20 MINUTES; COOK: 10 MINUTES; CHILL: 1 HOUR

FYI

The water for cooking pasta will come to a boil faster if you add the salt after the boiling begins. Also add a tablespoon of vegetable oil to keep the water from boiling over and the pasta from sticking together.

2½ cups rotini pasta, uncooked

1 cup sliced fresh mushrooms

½ cup freshly grated Parmesan cheese

½ cup commercial oil-free Italian dressing

¼ cup sliced green onions

¼ teaspoon coarsely ground pepper

½ large green pepper, seeded and cut into thin strips

½ large sweet red pepper, seeded and cut into thin strips

8 slices bacon, cooked and crumbled

1 Cook pasta according to package directions; drain. Rinse with cold water; place in a large bowl.

2 Add sliced mushrooms and next 6 ingredients to pasta; toss well. Cover and chill at least 1 hour.

3 Just before serving, add bacon to salad; toss gently. Serve immediately. Yield: 6 servings.

Note: To decrease preparation time and to add variety, substitute 2 tablespoons drained capers for bacon.

Italian Salad

PREP: 10 MINUTES; COOK: 10 MINUTES; CHILL: 1 HOUR

1 (12-ounce) package rotini pasta

2 (6-ounce) jars marinated artichoke hearts, undrained

1 (0.7-ounce) package Italian dressing mix

1 large green pepper, seeded and chopped

¼ pound hard salami, cut into ¼-inch strips

¾ cup sliced ripe olives

½ cup grated Parmesan cheese

¼ cup chopped fresh parsley

¼ cup chopped onion

1 Cook pasta according to package directions; drain. Rinse with cold water; drain.

2 Drain artichoke hearts, reserving ¼ cup marinade. (Reserve remaining marinade for another use.) Combine cooked pasta, artichoke hearts, reserved ¼ cup marinade, dressing mix, and remaining ingredients in a large bowl; toss gently. Cover and chill at least 1 hour. Toss salad before serving. Yield: 6 servings.

Mandarin Chicken Salad

PREP: 20 MINUTES; CHILL: 1 HOUR

3 cups chopped cooked chicken
1 cup diced celery
2 tablespoons lemon juice
1 tablespoon minced onion

⅓ cup mayonnaise
½ teaspoon salt
1 cup seedless green grapes
1 (2-ounce) package slivered
    almonds, toasted
1 (11-ounce) can mandarin
    oranges, drained
Lettuce leaves

1 Combine first 4 ingredients; cover and chill at least 1 hour.

2 Combine mayonnaise and salt. Add mayonnaise mixture, grapes, and almonds to chilled chicken mixture; toss gently. Stir in oranges. Serve chicken mixture on lettuce leaves. Yield: 6 servings.

Hot Turkey Salad

PREP: 10 MINUTES; COOK: 25 MINUTES

6 frozen puff pastry shells

2 cups diced cooked turkey
¾ cup thinly sliced celery
¾ cup mayonnaise
½ cup coarsely chopped almonds,
    toasted
2 tablespoons grated onion
1 tablespoon lemon juice
⅛ teaspoon pepper
1 pimiento, cut into thin strips

½ cup (2 ounces) shredded
    Cheddar cheese

1 Bake pastry shells according to package directions.

2 While pastry shells cook, combine turkey and next 7 ingredients in a saucepan. Cook over low heat until mixture is thoroughly heated, stirring often.

3 Fill prepared pastry shells with turkey mixture. Bake at 350° for 5 minutes. Sprinkle with cheese, and bake 5 additional minutes or until cheese melts. Serve immediately. Yield: 6 servings.

Peach-Plum Soup

PREP: 15 MINUTES; COOK: 15 MINUTES; CHILL: 3 HOURS

Before peeling peaches, dip the fruit into boiling water for 30 seconds; the skins will then slip off easily.

½ pound fresh peaches, peeled and sliced
½ pound fresh plums, peeled and sliced
1 cup plus 2 tablespoons sugar
2 cups dry red wine
1¾ cups water
1 (3-inch) stick cinnamon

1 teaspoon cornstarch
¼ cup water
½ cup whipping cream, whipped
Additional whipped cream (optional)
Ground cinnamon (optional)

1 Combine first 6 ingredients in a Dutch oven. Bring to a boil; reduce heat, and simmer, uncovered, 10 minutes or until fruit is tender. Remove and discard cinnamon stick. Transfer fruit mixture to a bowl.

2 Spoon 2 cups fruit mixture into container of an electric blender; cover and process until mixture is smooth, stopping once to scrape down sides. Transfer pureed mixture to Dutch oven. Repeat procedure using remaining half of fruit mixture.

3 Combine cornstarch and ¼ cup water, stirring until smooth. Bring pureed mixture to a boil. Stir cornstarch mixture into soup; boil, stirring constantly, 1 minute. Cover and chill at least 3 hours.

4 Stir whipped cream into soup, and ladle into bowls. If desired, dollop additional whipped cream on each serving, and sprinkle with ground cinnamon. Yield: 6 cups.

Peach-Plum Soup (facing page)

Cantaloupe Soup

PREP: 13 MINUTES

8 cups cubed cantaloupe (about 2 medium), chilled
¾ cup sweet white wine, chilled
¼ cup whipping cream

Garnish: fresh mint sprigs

1 Place half each of cantaloupe, white wine, and whipping cream in container of an electric blender; cover and process until smooth. Transfer pureed mixture to a large container. Repeat procedure using remaining cantaloupe, white wine, and whipping cream.

2 Ladle soup into bowls, and garnish, if desired. Yield: 7 cups.

Creamy Tomato Soup

1 (12-ounce) can evaporated milk

1 (10¾-ounce) can tomato soup, undiluted

1 (14½-ounce) can Italian stewed tomatoes, undrained and chopped

½ cup (2 ounces) shredded Cheddar cheese

6 slices bacon, cooked and broken in half

Garnish: fresh oregano sprigs

1 Combine milk and soup in a medium saucepan; add tomato and cheese. Cook over medium-low heat until cheese melts and mixture is thoroughly heated. Ladle soup into bowls, and top with bacon. Garnish, if desired. Yield: 4⅔ cups.

Taco Soup (facing page)

Taco Soup

PREP: 10 MINUTES; COOK: 22 MINUTES

1 pound ground chuck
1 large onion, chopped

3 (15½-ounce) cans Mexican-style chili beans, undrained
1 (15¼-ounce) can whole kernel corn, undrained
1 (15-ounce) can tomato sauce
1 (14½-ounce) can whole tomatoes, undrained and chopped
1 (4½-ounce) can chopped green chiles
1 (1¼-ounce) envelope taco seasoning mix
1 (1-ounce) envelope Ranch-style salad dressing mix
1½ cups water

Toppings: corn chips, shredded lettuce, chopped tomato, sour cream, shredded Cheddar cheese

1 Cook beef and onion in a Dutch oven over medium-high heat until meat is browned and onion is tender, stirring until meat crumbles; drain.

2 Stir beans and next 7 ingredients into beef mixture, and bring to a boil. Reduce heat, and simmer, uncovered, 15 minutes, stirring occasionally.

3 Spoon soup into bowls; top with desired toppings. Yield: 3½ quarts.

Use kitchen shears to chop canned whole tomatoes while they are still in the can.

Spicy Vegetable-Beef Soup

PREP: 15 MINUTES; COOK: 40 MINUTES

F Y I

Keep celery fresh and crisp by wrapping the stalks in paper towels and storing them in a plastic bag in the refrigerator. Make quick work of slicing celery by slicing three or four stalks at a time.

1 pound ground chuck
4 stalks celery, sliced
2 cloves garlic, pressed
1 medium onion, chopped

1 (30-ounce) jar chunky garden-style spaghetti sauce with mushrooms and peppers
1 (10½-ounce) can condensed beef broth, undiluted
2 cups water
1 teaspoon sugar
1 teaspoon salt
½ teaspoon freshly ground pepper

1 (16-ounce) package frozen mixed vegetables
1 (10-ounce) can diced tomatoes and green chiles

1 Cook first 4 ingredients in a Dutch oven over medium-high heat until meat is browned and vegetables are tender, stirring until meat crumbles; drain.

2 Stir spaghetti sauce and next 5 ingredients into beef mixture; bring to a boil. Cover, reduce heat, and simmer 15 minutes, stirring occasionally.

3 Add mixed vegetables and diced tomatoes and green chiles to beef mixture; return mixture to a boil. Cover and simmer 15 minutes or until vegetables are tender, stirring occasionally. Yield: 3 quarts.

Easy Brunswick Stew

PREP: 5 MINUTES; COOK: 20 MINUTES

1 (20-ounce) can Brunswick stew
1 (17-ounce) can lima beans, rinsed and drained
1 (11-ounce) can whole kernel corn, undrained
1 (10-ounce) can pork with barbecue sauce
1 (10-ounce) can barbecue beef
¾ cup water
¼ cup barbecue sauce
1 teaspoon lemon juice

1 Combine all ingredients in a Dutch oven; cover and cook over medium heat 20 minutes, stirring occasionally. Yield: 2 quarts.

Quick Chili with Beans

PREP: 8 MINUTES; COOK: 20 MINUTES

1 pound ground chuck
1 medium onion, chopped
1 clove garlic, minced

3 (8-ounce) cans tomato sauce
1 tablespoon chili powder
1 milk chocolate kiss
1 (15-ounce) can kidney beans,
  undrained
Shredded Cheddar cheese
  (optional)

1 Cook first 3 ingredients in a Dutch oven over medium-high heat until meat is browned and onion is tender, stirring until meat crumbles; drain.

2 Stir tomato sauce, chili powder, and chocolate kiss into beef mixture. Cook, uncovered, over low heat 15 minutes, stirring occasionally. Add beans, and cook until thoroughly heated. Ladle chili into bowls, and sprinkle with Cheddar cheese, if desired. Yield: 7 cups.

Shrimp Chowder

PREP: 12 MINUTES; COOK: 10 MINUTES

8 slices bacon

1 medium onion, chopped
1 medium-size green pepper,
  seeded and chopped
1 stalk celery, chopped

2 (10¾-ounce) cans cream of
  potato soup, undiluted
1 (10¾-ounce) can cream of
  celery soup, undiluted
2 (4¼-ounce) cans small shrimp,
  drained and rinsed
4 cups milk
¼ teaspoon pepper

1 Cook bacon in a Dutch oven until crisp; remove bacon, reserving 1 tablespoon drippings in Dutch oven. Crumble bacon, and set aside.

2 Cook onion, green pepper, and celery in drippings over medium heat, stirring constantly, until tender.

3 Add potato soup and remaining 4 ingredients to Dutch oven; cook 5 minutes or until thoroughly heated, stirring occasionally. Ladle chowder into bowls, and sprinkle with crumbled bacon. Yield: 2½ quarts.

Harvest Chowder

Harvest Chowder

PREP: 7 MINUTES; COOK: 7 MINUTES

4 slices bacon

2 stalks celery, thinly sliced
2 small carrots, scraped and
     thinly sliced
1 green onion, thinly sliced
1 (15-ounce) can cream-style corn
2 cups milk
2 cups cooked mashed potato
1 cup (4 ounces) shredded sharp
     Cheddar cheese
½ cup frozen English peas
¾ teaspoon salt

1 small tomato, cut into 8 slices
Freshly ground pepper

1 Cook bacon in a Dutch oven until crisp; remove bacon, reserving 1 tablespoon drippings in Dutch oven. Crumble bacon, and set aside.

2 Cook celery, carrot, and green onion in drippings over medium heat, stirring constantly, 5 minutes or until tender. Stir in corn and next 5 ingredients; cook, stirring constantly, until cheese melts.

3 Ladle chowder into bowls. Top each serving with a tomato slice. Sprinkle with crumbled bacon and pepper. Yield: 2 quarts.

Creamy Chicken-Vegetable Chowder

PREP: 5 MINUTES; COOK: 17 MINUTES

1 (11-ounce) can Mexican-style
    corn, undrained
1 (10¾-ounce) can cream of
    chicken soup, undiluted
1 (10¾-ounce) can cream of
    potato soup, undiluted
1 (4½-ounce) jar sliced
    mushrooms, undrained
1 (4½-ounce) can chopped green
    chiles, undrained
2 cups chopped cooked chicken
1½ cups milk
1 cup chicken broth
⅓ cup sliced green onions

1½ cups (6 ounces) shredded
    Cheddar cheese

1 Combine first 9 ingredients in a Dutch oven; cook over medium heat 15 minutes or until mixture is thoroughly heated, stirring occasionally.

2 Remove Dutch oven from heat; add cheese to chowder, stirring until cheese melts. Yield: 1¾ quarts.

Corn Chowder

PREP: 10 MINUTES; COOK: 25 MINUTES

6 slices bacon

1 cup chopped onion
2 medium-size round red
    potatoes, cubed
½ cup water

1 (15-ounce) can cream-style corn
1½ cups half-and-half
½ teaspoon salt
Dash of pepper

1 Cook bacon in a Dutch oven until crisp; remove bacon, reserving 2 tablespoons drippings in Dutch oven. Crumble bacon, and set aside.

2 Cook onion in drippings over medium heat, stirring constantly, until tender. Add potato and water; bring to a boil. Cover, reduce heat, and simmer 18 minutes or until potato is tender.

3 Stir corn and remaining 3 ingredients into potato mixture; cook until thoroughly heated, stirring often. Ladle into bowls, and sprinkle with bacon. Yield: 5 cups.

Grilled Pesto Sandwiches

PREP: 8 MINUTES; COOK: 5 MINUTES

1 (6-ounce) package sliced
   mozzarella cheese, cut into
   thirds
8 (1-inch-thick) slices Italian
   bread
¼ cup pizza sauce
¼ cup pesto sauce
20 slices pepperoni

2 tablespoons butter or
   margarine, softened
Garnish: additional pepperoni
   slices

1 Arrange 1 cheese slice on each of 4 slices of bread; spread evenly with pizza sauce. Top each with another cheese slice, and spread evenly with pesto sauce. Arrange 20 pepperoni slices over pesto sauce; top with remaining cheese slices and remaining bread slices.

2 Spread half of butter on tops of sandwiches. Invert sandwiches onto a hot nonstick skillet or griddle, and cook over medium heat until browned. Spread remaining butter on ungrilled sides of sandwiches; turn and cook until browned. Garnish, if desired. Serve immediately. Yield: 4 servings.

Grilled Pesto Sandwich

Pita Salad Sandwiches

PREP: 25 MINUTES

3 green onions, thinly sliced
2 small ripe avocados, peeled and
    sliced
2 medium tomatoes, coarsely
    chopped
2 stalks celery, thinly sliced
1 large cucumber, thinly sliced
1 medium-size green pepper,
    seeded and chopped
¼ teaspoon garlic powder
¼ teaspoon pepper

1 (8-ounce) bottle Italian
    dressing
6 (6-inch) pita bread rounds, cut
    in half crosswise
Plain low-fat yogurt (optional)

1 Combine first 8 ingredients in a large bowl.

2 Add dressing to vegetable mixture; toss gently. Spoon vegetable mixture evenly into pita halves. Top vegetable mixture with yogurt, if desired. Serve immediately. Yield: 6 servings.

FYI

Seed an avocado quickly by cutting it lengthwise all the way around the seed; twist the halves in opposite directions to separate. Insert the blade of a large knife into the seed, and twist it out.

Tuna Melts

PREP: 12 MINUTES; BROIL: 3 MINUTES

⅓ cup mayonnaise
¼ cup sliced pimiento-stuffed
    olives
3 tablespoons sweet pickle relish
2 tablespoons finely chopped
    onion
3 large hard-cooked eggs,
    chopped
1 (6-ounce) can solid white tuna
    in spring water, drained and
    flaked

3 English muffins, split and
    lightly toasted
1 (6-ounce) package sliced sharp
    Cheddar cheese

1 Combine first 6 ingredients.

2 Place muffin halves, cut sides up, on a baking sheet; spoon tuna mixture evenly onto muffin halves. Broil 5½ inches from heat (with electric oven door partially opened) 2 minutes. Top each muffin half with a cheese slice, and broil 1 additional minute or until cheese melts. Serve immediately. Yield: 6 servings.

Giant Meatball Sandwich

PREP: 8 MINUTES; COOK: 22 MINUTES

F⁄I

Place a metal colander upside down over the skillet while browning the meatballs for this recipe. This prevents splatters while allowing steam to escape.

1 pound ground chuck
½ pound ground pork sausage

2 cups spaghetti sauce with
    peppers and mushrooms
1 clove garlic, minced

1 (16-ounce) loaf unsliced Italian
    bread
1 (6-ounce) package sliced
    provolone cheese

1 Combine ground chuck and sausage; shape into 1-inch balls. Cook meatballs in a large skillet over medium-high heat 8 to 10 minutes or until browned. Drain meatballs on paper towels. Discard drippings.

2 Combine meatballs, spaghetti sauce, and garlic in skillet; bring to a boil. Reduce heat, and simmer, uncovered, 12 to 15 minutes or until meatballs are done, stirring mixture occasionally.

3 While sauce simmers, slice bread in half horizontally. Place bread, cut sides up, on a baking sheet. Broil 5½ inches from heat (with electric oven door partially opened) 1 to 2 minutes or until bread is lightly toasted. Spoon meatball mixture over bottom half of toasted bread; arrange cheese on top of meatballs, overlapping as needed. Cover with top of bread. Cut sandwich into 6 pieces, and serve immediately. Yield: 6 servings.

Giant Meatball Sandwich (facing page)

Hot Roast Beef Sandwiches

PREP: 15 MINUTES; BAKE: 25 MINUTES

1 (16-ounce) loaf unsliced Italian
  bread

½ cup finely chopped purple
  onion
½ cup chopped ripe olives
¼ cup mayonnaise
2 teaspoons Creole mustard

1 pound thinly sliced deli roast
  beef
1 (8-ounce) package sliced Swiss
  cheese

1 Place bread on a baking sheet; bake at 400° for 5 minutes. Slice bread in half horizontally.

2 Combine onion and next 3 ingredients; spread mixture on cut surfaces of bread.

3 Layer half each of beef and cheese on bottom half of bread; repeat layers with remaining beef and cheese. Cover with bread top. Cut sandwich into 4 pieces, and wrap each piece in aluminum foil. Bake at 400° for 20 minutes or until thoroughly heated. Yield: 4 servings.

Open-Faced Jalapeño Heroes

PREP: 14 MINUTES; COOK: 27 MINUTES

1 pound ground chuck

1 jalapeño pepper, seeded and
   chopped
1 (15-ounce) can tomato sauce,
   divided
1½ teaspoons dried oregano
⅛ teaspoon garlic powder

1 (16-ounce) loaf unsliced French
   bread
1 (8-ounce) jar process cheese
   spread with jalapeños
1 (4-ounce) can sliced
   mushrooms, drained
1 small onion, thinly sliced and
   separated into rings

1 cup (4 ounces) shredded
   mozzarella cheese

1 Brown ground chuck in a large skillet, stirring until it crumbles; drain.

2 Add jalapeño pepper and half of tomato sauce to beef; bring to a boil. Reduce heat, and simmer, uncovered, 5 minutes, stirring often. Add oregano and garlic powder; simmer 2 additional minutes, stirring often. Remove from heat.

3 Slice bread in half horizontally; place bread halves, cut sides up, on a baking sheet. Spread cut surfaces evenly with cheese spread. Top bread halves evenly with meat mixture, mushrooms, and onion rings. Drizzle remaining half of tomato sauce over both sandwich halves.

4 Bake, uncovered, at 325° for 15 minutes. Sprinkle with mozzarella cheese; bake 5 additional minutes or until cheese melts. Cut each half into 3 pieces, and serve immediately. Yield: 6 servings.

Smoked Sausage Sandwiches

PREP: 10 MINUTES; COOK: 20 MINUTES

1 pound smoked sausage, cut into ¼-inch-thick slices

2 medium tomatoes, peeled and cut into wedges

½ large onion, sliced and separated into rings

¾ cup green pepper strips

¼ teaspoon salt

¼ teaspoon dried oregano

6 (6-inch) French rolls, split horizontally

½ cup (2 ounces) shredded mozzarella cheese

1 Cook sausage in a skillet over medium heat until browned; remove sausage, reserving 1 tablespoon drippings in skillet. Set sausage aside. Cook tomato, onion, and green pepper in drippings, stirring constantly, until tender. Stir in sausage, salt, and oregano.

2 Spoon sausage mixture evenly over bottom halves of rolls; top evenly with cheese. Cover with tops of rolls. Bake at 400° for 10 minutes or until cheese melts. Yield: 6 servings.

Double-Decker Club Sandwiches

PREP: 18 MINUTES

½ cup sour cream

1½ tablespoons prepared horseradish

1 teaspoon honey mustard

⅛ teaspoon garlic salt

Dash of ground white pepper

¾ pound thinly sliced cooked ham

12 slices whole wheat bread, toasted

4 (1-ounce) slices Swiss cheese

8 leaf lettuce leaves, divided

¾ pound sliced cooked turkey

8 tomato slices

4 slices bacon, cooked

16 pimiento-stuffed olives

1 Combine first 5 ingredients.

2 Layer ham evenly on 4 slices of bread. Top each with 1 heaping teaspoon sour cream mixture, 1 slice cheese, 1 lettuce leaf, and another slice of bread. Layer turkey evenly over sandwiches, and top each with 1 heaping teaspoon sour cream mixture, 1 lettuce leaf, 2 tomato slices, and 1 slice of bacon. Top with remaining slices of bread.

3 Skewer an olive onto each of 16 wooden picks. Cut each sandwich into 4 triangles, and secure each triangle with a pick. Yield: 4 servings.

FYI

Leaving the peel on the tomatoes saves time as well as nutrients.

Asparagus Grill Sandwiches

PREP: 10 MINUTES; COOK: 25 MINUTES

FYI

Choose asparagus stalks that are uniform in size to ensure even cooking. Thin stalks are generally more tender.

16 fresh asparagus spears

4 thin slices onion

8 slices sandwich bread
Butter or margarine
8 slices cooked ham or 16 slices bacon, cooked
4 (1-ounce) slices process American cheese

4 slices tomato
Cheddar Cheese Sauce (facing page)
Paprika (optional)

1 Snap off tough ends of asparagus. Remove scales from stalks with a knife or vegetable peeler, if desired. Cook asparagus, covered, in a small amount of boiling water 6 to 8 minutes or until crisp-tender. Drain and set aside.

2 While asparagus is cooking, place onion on a moderately hot griddle; cook 1 minute on each side or until browned. Remove onion from griddle, and set aside.

3 Spread one side of each bread slice with butter. Place 4 slices of bread, buttered side down, on griddle. Layer each bread slice with 2 slices of ham or 4 slices of bacon, and 1 slice of cheese. Place remaining 4 slices bread, buttered side up, on top of cheese. Cook until sandwiches are golden on bottom; turn and cook other side until browned.

4 To serve, place sandwiches on individual plates. Top each sandwich with 1 slice each of onion and tomato and 4 asparagus spears. Spoon Cheddar Cheese Sauce over sandwiches. Sprinkle with paprika, if desired, and serve immediately. Yield: 4 servings.

Asparagus Grill Sandwich

Cheddar Cheese Sauce

2 tablespoons butter or margarine
2 tablespoons all-purpose flour
1 cup milk
1 cup (4 ounces) shredded sharp
    Cheddar cheese

1 Melt butter in a heavy saucepan over low heat; add flour, stirring until mixture is smooth. Cook, stirring constantly, 1 minute. Gradually add milk; cook over medium heat, stirring constantly, until mixture is thickened and bubbly. Add Cheddar cheese, and stir until cheese melts. Yield: 1½ cups.

Once you've chosen the entrée for a meal, your thoughts turn to what you should serve with it. Our array of quick side dishes will stand up to the main course and take the ho-hum out of mealtime in the blink of an eye. That's

SIDE DISHES

about how long it takes to prepare fresh vegetables like **PEACH-GLAZED CARROTS**, pasta favorites like **NOODLES ROMANOFF**, or trendy grains like **BASIL AND TOMATO COUSCOUS**. Go ahead—fix a special entrée *and* a special side dish. You won't spend any extra time in the kitchen.

Baked Cheddar Tomatoes (page 159), Orzo Primavera (page 164)

151

Asparagus with Orange-Butter Sauce

1½ pounds fresh asparagus

⅓ cup butter or margarine
2 tablespoons grated orange rind
¼ cup orange juice

Garnish: orange slices

1 Snap off tough ends of asparagus. Remove scales from stalks with a knife or vegetable peeler, if desired. Arrange asparagus in a steamer basket over boiling water; cover and steam 7 minutes or until asparagus is crisp-tender.

2 While asparagus steams, combine butter, orange rind, and juice in a saucepan. Bring to a boil over high heat; reduce heat to medium, and cook, uncovered, until mixture is reduced by half and slightly thickened, stirring occasionally.

3 Arrange asparagus in a serving dish; pour sauce over asparagus. Garnish, if desired. Yield: 6 servings.

Broccoli with Garlic-Lemon Sauce

PREP: 7 MINUTES; COOK: 10 MINUTES

1½ pounds fresh broccoli

1 clove garlic, minced
2 tablespoons olive oil
2 tablespoons lemon juice

1 Remove broccoli leaves, and cut off tough ends of stalks; discard. Wash broccoli; cut into spears. Arrange in a steamer basket over boiling water; cover and steam 6 minutes or until crisp-tender.

2 While broccoli steams, cook garlic in hot oil in a skillet over medium-high heat, stirring constantly, until tender. Stir in lemon juice.

3 Arrange broccoli in a dish; pour sauce over broccoli. Yield: 4 servings.

Easy Orange Broccoli

PREP: **7** MINUTES; COOK: **10** MINUTES

1 pound fresh broccoli flowerets

1 tablespoon butter or margarine
1 tablespoon all-purpose flour
1 tablespoon grated orange rind
¾ cup orange juice

Grated orange rind (optional)

1 Arrange broccoli in a steamer basket over boiling water. Cover and steam 4 to 5 minutes or until broccoli is crisp-tender; drain.

2 While broccoli steams, melt butter in a heavy saucepan over low heat; add flour, stirring until smooth. Cook, stirring constantly, 1 minute. Gradually add 1 tablespoon orange rind and orange juice. Cook over medium heat, stirring constantly, until thickened and bubbly.

3 Arrange broccoli in a serving dish; pour sauce over broccoli. Sprinkle with grated orange rind, if desired. Yield: 4 servings.

F/I

Grate the rind while the orange is whole, and then cut the orange in half to juice it.

Minted Baby Carrots

PREP: **5** MINUTES; COOK: **15** MINUTES

4 cups baby carrots

3 tablespoons butter or margarine
¼ cup finely chopped fresh mint
    leaves
2 tablespoons sugar

Garnish: fresh mint sprigs

1 Arrange carrots in a steamer basket over boiling water. Cover and steam 7 minutes; drain.

2 While carrots steam, melt butter in a large skillet over low heat. Stir in chopped mint and sugar. Add carrots, and cook 5 to 7 minutes or until carrots are crisp-tender and well glazed, stirring occasionally.

3 Spoon carrots into a serving dish. Garnish, if desired. Yield: 6 servings.

Peach-Glazed Carrots

PREP: 2 MINUTES; COOK: 10 MINUTES

FYI

Cut carrots into uniform pieces so they'll cook evenly. Cook them in as little water as possible to minimize nutrient loss.

1 pound carrots, scraped and sliced

⅓ cup peach preserves
1 tablespoon butter or margarine, melted

1 Cook carrot in a small amount of boiling water 5 to 6 minutes or until crisp-tender. Drain and return to pan.

2 Combine peach preserves and butter; add to carrot. Cook over low heat until thoroughly heated, stirring occasionally. Yield: 4 servings.

Creamed Fresh Corn

PREP: 10 MINUTES; COOK: 11 MINUTES

FYI

Remove silks from fresh corn by rubbing downward toward the stalk end with a damp paper towel or by brushing the ear with a vegetable brush under cold running water.

4 ears fresh corn
1 teaspoon sugar (optional)

¼ cup butter or margarine, melted
⅓ cup whipping cream
¼ teaspoon salt
½ teaspoon freshly ground pepper

1 Remove husks and silks from corn. Cut corn from cobs, scraping cobs well to remove all milk. Stir in sugar, if desired.

2 Cook corn in butter in a medium saucepan over medium heat, stirring constantly, 1 minute. Gradually stir in whipping cream; cook 10 to 12 minutes or until liquid is absorbed, stirring often. Stir in salt and pepper. Serve immediately. Yield: 2 cups.

Parmesan Corn on the Cob

Parmesan Corn on the Cob

PREP: 12 MINUTES; MICROWAVE: 10 MINUTES

¼ cup butter or margarine, melted

¼ cup grated Parmesan cheese

½ teaspoon dried Italian seasoning

4 ears fresh corn, husks and silks removed

1 Combine first 3 ingredients; set mixture aside.

2 Wrap each ear of corn in heavy-duty plastic wrap, and place on a microwave-safe plate. Microwave at HIGH 10 to 13 minutes or until tender, rearranging corn once. Unwrap corn, and spread butter mixture over each ear. Yield: 4 servings.

Note: To prepare corn in a conventional oven, wrap it in heavy-duty aluminum foil; then bake at 500° for 20 minutes or until tender.

Green Beans with Buttered Pecans

PREP: 10 MINUTES; COOK: 15 MINUTES

FYI

Select young, tender green beans. Trim the stem end only, leaving the pointed end to enhance the appearance of the beans. (Find the photo for this recipe on page 114.)

½ pound fresh green beans
2½ cups water
¼ teaspoon salt

2 tablespoons coarsely chopped pecans
1 tablespoon butter or margarine, melted
⅛ teaspoon pepper

1 Wash beans; trim stem ends, and remove strings. Combine water and salt in a medium saucepan; bring to a boil. Add beans; cook, uncovered, 10 minutes or just until crisp-tender. Drain.

2 While beans cook, cook pecans in butter in a large skillet over medium heat, stirring constantly, until golden. Add beans; cook until thoroughly heated, tossing gently. Spoon into a serving dish, and sprinkle with pepper. Yield: 2 servings.

Mushroom-Bacon Green Beans

PREP: 10 MINUTES; COOK: 15 MINUTES

2 (10-ounce) packages frozen cut green beans

4 slices bacon

1 medium onion, chopped
½ pound fresh mushrooms, sliced
¾ teaspoon salt
⅛ teaspoon pepper

1 Cook beans according to package directions.

2 While beans are cooking, cook bacon in a large skillet until crisp. Remove bacon, reserving 1 tablespoon drippings in skillet. Crumble bacon, and set aside.

3 Add onion and mushrooms to drippings; cook over medium-high heat, stirring constantly, until tender. Add beans, salt, and pepper; cook until thoroughly heated. Spoon bean mixture into a serving dish; sprinkle with bacon. Yield: 6 servings.

Sautéed Sweet Peppers

PREP: **7** MINUTES; COOK: **4** MINUTES

1 large sweet red pepper
1 large sweet yellow pepper
1 large green pepper
1 teaspoon chopped fresh thyme
    or ½ teaspoon dried thyme
1 tablespoon butter or margarine,
    melted
Garnish: fresh thyme sprigs

1 Seed peppers, and cut into 1-inch pieces. Cook pepper pieces and chopped thyme in butter in a large skillet over medium-high heat, stirring constantly, 4 minutes or until tender. Spoon into a serving dish; garnish, if desired. Yield: 5 servings.

You can use any color combination of sweet peppers if you can't find all three colors. (Find the photo for this recipe on page 102.)

Creamy Potato Bake

PREP: **10** MINUTES; BAKE: **25** MINUTES

2 (2.1-ounce) packages instant
    mashed potatoes

½ cup softened cream cheese
1½ tablespoons butter or
    margarine
1 large egg
1 green onion, finely chopped

Paprika

1 Prepare potatoes according to package directions.

2 Add cream cheese and butter to prepared potatoes; beat with an electric mixer until blended. Add egg and green onion; beat well.

3 Spoon potato mixture into a greased 1-quart baking dish; sprinkle with paprika. Bake at 400° for 25 minutes or until thoroughly heated. Yield: 4 servings.

Oven-Roasted Potatoes

PREP: 5 MINUTES; BAKE: 27 MINUTES

1 large onion, chopped
2 cloves garlic, minced
1 tablespoon olive oil

½ cup chopped sweet red pepper
½ teaspoon salt
¼ teaspoon pepper
¼ teaspoon hot sauce

3 cups unpeeled cubed potato
2 tablespoons butter or margarine

1 Cook onion and garlic in hot oil in a 10-inch cast iron skillet over medium heat, stirring constantly, until tender.

2 Stir chopped red pepper and next 3 ingredients into onion mixture; cook, stirring constantly, 2 minutes.

3 Stir potato and butter into onion mixture. Bake, uncovered, at 400° for 20 minutes or until potato is tender. Yield: 4 servings.

Oven-Roasted Potatoes

Baked Cheddar Tomatoes

PREP: **7** MINUTES; BAKE: **12** MINUTES

5 medium tomatoes, cut in half
    crosswise
¾ teaspoon salt

1 cup soft breadcrumbs
1 cup (4 ounces) shredded
    Cheddar cheese
¼ cup butter or margarine,
    melted
1 teaspoon dried basil
¼ teaspoon ground red pepper

Garnish: fresh basil sprigs

1 Sprinkle cut sides of tomato halves with salt. Place tomato halves, cut sides up, on a baking sheet.

2 Combine breadcrumbs and next 4 ingredients; spread evenly over tomato halves.

3 Bake at 350° for 12 to 15 minutes or until tomatoes are thoroughly heated and cheese melts. Arrange on a serving platter, and garnish, if desired. Yield: 10 servings.

Zucchini Toss

PREP: **10** MINUTES; COOK: **5** MINUTES

1 pound medium zucchini, cut
    into ¼-inch-thick slices
1½ teaspoons olive oil

1 tablespoon freshly grated
    Parmesan cheese
¼ teaspoon grated lemon rind
¼ teaspoon salt
¼ teaspoon pepper

1 Cook zucchini in hot oil in a large skillet over medium-high heat, stirring constantly, 5 minutes or until crisp-tender. Remove from heat; cover and let stand 5 minutes.

2 Combine cheese and remaining 3 ingredients. Spoon zucchini into a serving dish, and sprinkle with cheese mixture; toss gently. Serve immediately. Yield: 3 servings.

Golden Apples

PREP: 5 MINUTES; COOK: 8 MINUTES

Before measuring honey, spray the measuring spoon or cup with vegetable cooking spray. The honey will slide right out.

1 Granny Smith apple, cored and cut into ¼-inch-thick slices
2 Rome apples, cored and cut into ¼-inch-thick slices
½ cup orange juice

¼ cup honey
2 tablespoons apricot preserves

1 Combine apple slices and orange juice in a large skillet; bring to a boil over high heat.

2 Stir honey and apricot preserves into apple mixture; reduce heat, and simmer, uncovered, 4 to 5 minutes or until apple is tender. Serve warm. Yield: 4 servings.

Chafing Dish Fruit

PREP: 5 MINUTES; COOK: 20 MINUTES

1 (20-ounce) can unsweetened pineapple slices
1 (16-ounce) can apricot halves in extra-light syrup
1 (16-ounce) can peach halves in extra-light syrup
1 (16-ounce) can pear halves in extra-light syrup

1 cup pitted prunes
1 tablespoon grated orange rind
1 teaspoon grated lemon rind
⅔ cup orange juice
1 tablespoon lemon juice

1 Drain first 4 ingredients, reserving juices in a bowl. Combine fruit in a Dutch oven. Stir juice mixture; set aside 2½ cups. Reserve remaining juice mixture for another use.

2 Add reserved 2½ cups juice mixture, prunes, and remaining ingredients to fruit mixture in Dutch oven. Bring to a boil; reduce heat, and simmer, uncovered, 20 minutes. Transfer fruit mixture to a chafing dish; serve warm. Yield: 8 servings.

Fruit Kabobs

Fruit Kabobs

PREP: 18 MINUTES

24 fresh strawberries
24 seedless green grapes
24 fresh pineapple chunks
24 large fresh blackberries

½ cup marshmallow creme
½ cup mayonnaise
2 teaspoons grated orange rind
1 teaspoon ground ginger
Garnish: grated orange rind

1 Alternately thread first 4 ingredients onto 12 (12-inch) bamboo skewers; cover and chill, if desired.

2 Combine marshmallow creme and next 3 ingredients. Spoon into a serving bowl; garnish, if desired. Serve marshmallow creme mixture with kabobs. Yield: 12 kabobs.

Note: Toss the fruit mixture with the marshmallow creme mixture, and serve it as a salad, if desired.

Tomato-Garlic Pasta

PREP: 10 MINUTES; COOK: 18 MINUTES

FYI

Hard cheeses like Parmesan and Romano are easiest to grate at room temperature. For easy cleanup, lightly brush the grater with oil or spray with vegetable cooking spray before grating.

12 ounces dried angel hair pasta, uncooked

3 large cloves garlic, chopped
1 tablespoon olive oil

3 large tomatoes, peeled, seeded, and diced
½ cup dry white wine
¼ cup firmly packed fresh basil leaves, cut into ¼-inch-wide strips
3 to 4 tablespoons balsamic vinegar
1 teaspoon freshly ground pepper
¼ teaspoon salt

1 cup grated Parmesan cheese

1 Cook pasta according to package directions; drain.

2 While pasta cooks, cook garlic in hot oil in a large skillet over medium heat, stirring constantly, until lightly browned.

3 Add tomato and next 5 ingredients to skillet; bring to a boil. Reduce heat, and simmer, uncovered, 5 minutes, stirring occasionally.

4 Spoon tomato mixture over pasta; sprinkle with cheese. Serve immediately. Yield: 8 servings.

Creamy Fettuccine

PREP: 5 MINUTES; COOK: 23 MINUTES

6 ounces dried fettuccine, uncooked

¼ cup butter or margarine
2 tablespoons all-purpose flour
½ cup water
½ cup half-and-half
½ cup freshly grated Parmesan cheese
2 teaspoons dried parsley flakes
½ teaspoon garlic powder
½ teaspoon poppy seeds
½ teaspoon coarsely ground pepper
¼ teaspoon salt

1 Cook pasta according to package directions, omitting salt; drain.

2 While pasta cooks, melt butter in a large saucepan over low heat; add flour, stirring until smooth. Cook, stirring constantly, 1 minute. Gradually add water and half-and-half; cook over medium heat, stirring constantly, until mixture is thickened and bubbly. Stir in cheese and remaining 5 ingredients. Add pasta; toss well. Serve immediately. Yield: 3 servings.

Spinach-Pesto Pasta

PREP: 10 MINUTES; COOK: 10 MINUTES

1 (12-ounce) package linguine

1 (10-ounce) package frozen
    chopped spinach, thawed
½ cup grated Parmesan cheese
⅓ cup packed fresh basil leaves
¼ cup pine nuts, toasted
2 tablespoons butter or
    margarine, softened
1 teaspoon crushed garlic
½ teaspoon coarsely ground
    pepper
¼ teaspoon salt
¼ teaspoon anise seeds, ground

½ cup olive oil

1 Cook pasta according to package directions; drain.

2 While pasta cooks, drain spinach, pressing between layers of paper towels to remove excess moisture. Position knife blade in food processor bowl; add spinach, Parmesan cheese, and next 7 ingredients. Process 30 seconds, stopping once to scrape down sides.

3 Pour oil through food chute with processor running, processing just until mixture is smooth. Combine spinach mixture and pasta, tossing gently. Serve pasta immediately. Yield: 8 servings.

Spinach-Pesto Pasta

Noodles Romanoff

PREP: **5** MINUTES; COOK: **30** MINUTES

1 (8-ounce) package wide egg
  noodles

1 (16-ounce) carton sour cream
¼ cup butter or margarine,
  melted
¼ teaspoon salt
¼ teaspoon pepper
1 clove garlic, pressed
¼ cup grated Parmesan cheese

Chopped fresh parsley

1 Cook noodles according to package directions; drain.

2 Stir sour cream and next 4 ingredients into noodles; spoon into a greased 2-quart baking dish. Sprinkle with cheese.

3 Cover and bake at 350° for 20 minutes or until thoroughly heated. Sprinkle with parsley just before serving. Yield: 6 servings.

Orzo Primavera

PREP: **7** MINUTES; COOK: **14** MINUTES

FYI

Orzo is tiny rice-shaped pasta. It cooks quickly and is available in most supermarkets.

1 pound fresh asparagus

3 quarts water
2 teaspoons salt
2 cups orzo, uncooked

½ cup chopped sweet red pepper
3 cloves garlic, minced
1 tablespoon olive oil
1 cup frozen English peas, thawed
½ cup chicken broth
1 teaspoon grated lemon rind
¼ teaspoon ground white pepper

½ cup freshly grated Parmesan
  cheese

1 Snap off tough ends of asparagus. Remove scales from stalks with a knife or vegetable peeler, if desired. Cut into 1-inch pieces; set aside.

2 Bring water and salt to a boil in a Dutch oven. Add orzo; cook 5 minutes. Add asparagus; cook 4 minutes. Drain.

3 Cook red pepper and garlic in hot oil in a large skillet over medium-high heat, stirring constantly, until crisp-tender. Add peas; cook, stirring constantly, 1 minute. Add broth, rind, and white pepper; bring to a boil. Cook 1 minute.

4 Combine pepper mixture and orzo mixture in a large bowl; sprinkle with cheese. Yield: 8 servings.

Parslied Rice

PREP: 1 MINUTE; COOK: 29 MINUTES

3 cups water
1 tablespoon chicken-flavored
     bouillon granules
1½ cups regular long-grain rice,
     uncooked

⅓ cup sliced green onions
2 tablespoons butter or
     margarine, melted
½ cup chopped fresh parsley

1 Combine water and bouillon granules in a large saucepan; bring to a boil. Stir in rice; return to a boil. Cover, reduce heat, and simmer 25 minutes or until rice is tender and liquid is absorbed.

2 While rice cooks, cook green onions in melted butter in a small skillet over medium heat, stirring constantly, until tender. Combine cooked rice, green onions, and parsley; toss gently. Yield: 6 servings.

Raisin Rice with Curry

PREP: 14 MINUTES; COOK: 5 MINUTES

¼ cup chopped onion
2 tablespoons butter or
     margarine, melted

1 cup water
1 teaspoon chicken-flavored
     bouillon granules
½ teaspoon curry powder
1 cup quick long-grain rice,
     uncooked
¼ cup raisins

1 Cook onion in butter in a medium saucepan over medium heat, stirring constantly, until tender.

2 Stir water, bouillon granules, and curry powder into onion mixture; bring to a boil. Stir in rice and raisins. Cover, remove from heat, and let stand 10 minutes or until rice is tender and liquid is absorbed. Stir gently with a fork before serving. Yield: 3 servings.

Hot Pepper Rice

Hot Pepper Rice

PREP: 6 MINUTES; BAKE: 15 MINUTES

3 cups cooked long-grain rice
1 (8-ounce) carton sour cream
1 (4½-ounce) can chopped green
 chiles, drained
1 fresh jalapeño pepper, seeded
 and diced

1 cup (4 ounces) shredded
 Monterey Jack cheese,
 divided
1 cup (4 ounces) shredded
 Cheddar cheese, divided

1 Combine first 4 ingredients. Spoon half of mixture into a lightly greased 1½-quart baking dish.

2 Sprinkle ½ cup each of Monterey Jack cheese and Cheddar cheese over rice mixture in dish. Repeat layers using remaining rice mixture and cheeses. Bake, uncovered, at 350° for 15 minutes or until mixture is thoroughly heated. Yield: 6 servings.

Seasoned Rice

PREP: 10 MINUTES; COOK: 5 MINUTES

1¼ cups canned chicken broth,
    undiluted
1 tablespoon butter or margarine
1 tablespoon soy sauce
¼ teaspoon celery seeds
¼ teaspoon dried parsley flakes
⅛ teaspoon dried basil
⅛ teaspoon ground thyme
⅛ teaspoon pepper

1½ cups quick long-grain rice,
    uncooked

1 Combine first 8 ingredients in a large saucepan; bring to a boil.

2 Stir rice into broth mixture; cover, remove from heat, and let stand 5 minutes. Stir gently with a fork before serving. Yield: 6 servings.

Dressed-Up Wild Rice

PREP: 5 MINUTES; COOK: 20 MINUTES

1 cup sliced fresh mushrooms
3 green onions, sliced
1 tablespoon butter, melted

1 (6.2-ounce package) quick
    long-grain and wild rice mix
    (including seasoning packet),
    uncooked
1⅔ cups water
⅓ cup sherry

1 Cook mushrooms and green onions in butter in a large skillet over medium-high heat, stirring constantly, until tender.

2 Stir rice mix, seasoning packet, water, and sherry into vegetable mixture; bring to a boil, stirring occasionally. Cover, reduce heat, and simmer 10 minutes or until rice is tender and liquid is absorbed. Stir gently with a fork before serving. Yield: 4 servings.

Wild Rice with Vegetables

PREP: 5 MINUTES; COOK: 12 MINUTES

2 green onions, thinly sliced
1 tablespoon butter or margarine, melted

1 (6.2-ounce) package quick long-grain and wild rice mix, uncooked
1 (10¾-ounce) can chicken broth, undiluted
⅔ cup water

1 (6-ounce) package frozen snow pea pods, thawed and drained
4 large fresh mushrooms, sliced
1 (8-ounce) can sliced water chestnuts, drained
1 tablespoon vegetable oil

1 Cook green onions in butter in a large skillet over medium-high heat, stirring constantly, until tender.

2 Stir rice mix, broth, and water into green onions. (Reserve seasoning packet for another use.) Bring to a boil; cover, reduce heat, and simmer 10 minutes or until rice is tender and liquid is absorbed.

3 While rice mix cooks, cook snow peas, mushrooms, and water chestnuts in hot oil 2 minutes; stir into rice mixture. Yield: 6 servings.

Wild Rice with Vegetables

Basil and Tomato Couscous

PREP: 20 MINUTES; CHILL: 2 HOURS

1¼ cups boiling water
1¼ cups couscous, uncooked

1 cup finely chopped fresh basil
⅓ cup finely chopped purple
    onion
3 slices bacon, cooked and
    crumbled
2 medium tomatoes, seeded and
    chopped

¼ cup cider vinegar
2 tablespoons olive oil
¼ teaspoon salt
¼ teaspoon pepper

1 Combine boiling water and couscous in a large bowl; cover and let stand 5 minutes. Uncover and fluff with a fork; let cool slightly.

2 Add basil and next 3 ingredients to couscous; stir well.

3 Combine vinegar and remaining 3 ingredients in a jar; cover tightly, and shake vigorously. Drizzle vinegar mixture over couscous mixture, and toss gently. Cover and chill at least 2 hours. Toss gently before serving. Yield: 6 servings.

Couscous (koos-koos) is a tiny, bead-shaped pasta that cooks quickly. Look for it alongside rice and grains at the supermarket.

Garlic-Cheese Grits

PREP: 1 MINUTE; COOK: 12 MINUTES

4 cups water
1 cup quick-cooking grits,
    uncooked
½ teaspoon salt

1 (6-ounce) roll process cheese
    food with garlic
⅛ teaspoon ground red pepper

1 Bring water to a boil in a Dutch oven; stir in grits and salt. Return to a boil; cover, reduce heat, and simmer 5 minutes, stirring occasionally.

2 Remove from heat; add cheese and pepper, stirring until cheese melts. Yield: 6 servings.

Even if you're short on time, you can include warm, fresh-baked bread on the menu. Our quick-as-a-wink recipes let you serve breads that look and taste exceptional. They use time-saving ingredients like

BREADS

self-rising flour, biscuit and baking mix, rapid-rise yeast, and commercial bread. We've even tossed in a bread machine recipe. With so many conveniences built into these recipes, you can have homemade bread any night of the week.

Sour Cream Yeast Rolls (page 181), Parmesan Twists (page 175)

Flaky Buttermilk Biscuits

PREP: 8 MINUTES; BAKE: 8 MINUTES

F/I

Roll or pat the dough into an 8- x 6-inch rectangle. Then cut the dough into 2-inch squares with a sharp knife instead of using a biscuit cutter. You'll decrease prep time and eliminate any leftover dough.

½ cup butter or margarine
2 cups self-rising flour
¾ cup buttermilk

Butter or margarine, melted

1 Cut ½ cup butter into flour with a pastry blender until mixture is crumbly. Add buttermilk, stirring with a fork just until flour is moistened. Turn dough out onto a lightly floured surface, and knead gently 4 or 5 times.

2 Roll or pat dough to ¾-inch thickness; cut with a 2-inch biscuit cutter. Place biscuits on a lightly greased baking sheet; bake at 450° for 8 to 10 minutes or until golden. Remove biscuits from oven, and brush with melted butter. Yield: 16 biscuits.

Cream Cheese Biscuits

PREP: 8 MINUTES; BAKE: 8 MINUTES

F/I

Using self-rising flour saves time because it already contains salt and baking powder. If you don't have it on hand, just add 1½ teaspoons baking powder and ½ teaspoon salt to 1 cup all-purpose flour, and stir well.

1 (3-ounce) package cream cheese
¼ cup butter or margarine
2½ cups self-rising flour
¾ cup milk

1 Cut cream cheese and butter into flour with a pastry blender until mixture is crumbly. Add milk, stirring with a fork just until flour is moistened. Turn dough out onto a lightly floured surface, and knead gently 4 or 5 times.

2 Roll dough to ½-inch thickness; cut with a 2-inch biscuit cutter. Place biscuits on a lightly greased baking sheet; bake at 425° for 8 to 10 minutes or until biscuits are golden. Yield: 16 biscuits.

Lightnin' Cheese Biscuits

PREP: 8 MINUTES; BAKE: 8 MINUTES

2 cups biscuit and baking mix
⅔ cup (2.6 ounces) finely
    shredded Cheddar cheese
½ cup water

1 Combine all ingredients, stirring with a fork just until dry ingredients are moistened. Turn dough out onto a lightly floured surface, and knead gently 7 or 8 times.

2 Roll or pat dough to ½-inch thickness; cut with a 2½-inch biscuit cutter. Place on a lightly greased baking sheet; bake at 450° for 8 to 10 minutes or until golden. Yield: 9 biscuits.

Blueberry Muffins with Streusel Topping

PREP: 12 MINUTES; BAKE: 18 MINUTES

2 cups self-rising flour
⅓ cup sugar

1 large egg, lightly beaten
¾ cup milk
¼ cup vegetable oil

1 cup fresh or frozen blueberries

¼ cup firmly packed brown sugar
2 tablespoons self-rising flour
1 tablespoon butter or margarine

1 Combine 2 cups flour and ⅓ cup sugar in a large bowl; set aside 2 tablespoons flour mixture. Make a well in center of remaining mixture.

2 Combine egg, milk, and oil; add to dry ingredients in bowl. Stir just until dry ingredients are moistened.

3 Combine blueberries and reserved 2 tablespoons flour mixture; toss gently. Fold blueberries into batter; spoon into greased muffin pans, filling three-fourths full.

4 Combine brown sugar and 2 tablespoons flour; cut in butter with a pastry blender until mixture is crumbly. Sprinkle mixture over batter. Bake at 400° for 18 minutes or until lightly browned. Remove from pans immediately. Yield: 1 dozen.

FYI

Coat fruit and nuts lightly with flour before you stir them into muffin or cake batter to keep them from sinking to the bottom.

Chive Muffins

PREP: 6 MINUTES; BAKE: 18 MINUTES

2 cups all-purpose flour
1 tablespoon baking powder
½ teaspoon salt
1 tablespoon sugar
1 tablespoon brown sugar

1 large egg, lightly beaten
1 cup milk
¼ cup chopped fresh or
    freeze-dried chives
¼ cup butter or margarine,
    melted

1 Combine first 5 ingredients in a medium bowl; make a well in center of mixture.

2 Combine egg and remaining 3 ingredients; add to dry ingredients. Stir just until dry ingredients are moistened.

3 Spoon batter into greased muffin pans, filling two-thirds full. Bake at 400° for 18 to 20 minutes or until lightly browned. Remove from pans immediately. Yield: 1 dozen.

Chive Muffins

Pumpkin-Molasses Muffins

PREP: 10 MINUTES; BAKE: 20 MINUTES

½ cup butter or margarine,
    softened
¾ cup firmly packed brown sugar
1 cup canned pumpkin
¼ cup molasses
1 large egg

1¾ cups self-rising flour
¾ teaspoon baking soda
¼ cup chopped pecans

1 Beat butter at medium speed of an electric mixer until creamy; add sugar, beating well. Add pumpkin, molasses, and egg; beat well.

2 Combine flour and soda; add to butter mixture. Stir until dry ingredients are moistened. Stir in pecans.

3 Spoon batter into greased muffin pans, filling two-thirds full. Bake at 375° for 20 minutes. Remove from pans immediately. Yield: 15 muffins.

FYI

Grease muffin pans quickly with vegetable cooking spray. Or use paper baking cups instead if you want to cut cleanup time.

Parmesan Twists

PREP: 26 MINUTES; BAKE: 10 MINUTES

¼ cup butter or margarine,
    softened
1 cup grated Parmesan cheese
½ cup sour cream

1 cup all-purpose flour
½ teaspoon dried Italian
    seasoning

1 egg yolk, lightly beaten
1 tablespoon water
Poppy seeds

1 Beat butter at medium speed of an electric mixer until creamy; add cheese and sour cream; beat well.

2 Combine flour and Italian seasoning. Gradually add to butter mixture, stirring until smooth.

3 Turn dough out onto a lightly floured surface; divide dough in half. Roll each portion of dough into a 12- x 7-inch rectangle; cut into 6- x ½-inch strips. Twist each strip 2 or 3 times, and place on a lightly greased baking sheet.

4 Combine yolk and water; brush over strips. Sprinkle with poppy seeds. Bake at 350° for 10 minutes or until golden. Yield: 4½ dozen.

FYI

This dough bakes into thin and crispy little breadsticks. You don't have to worry about rising time with these twists—they contain no yeast.

Country Corn Sticks

PREP: 13 MINUTES; BAKE: 15 MINUTES

FYI

You'll give these corn sticks a crisp brown crust if you preheat well-greased cast-iron pans until they are so hot they almost smoke. Just put the pans in the oven when you turn it on; they'll heat up as the oven does.

1¼ cups cornmeal
¾ cup all-purpose flour
1 tablespoon baking powder
¾ teaspoon salt
1 tablespoon sugar

2 large eggs, lightly beaten
1 cup milk
¼ cup vegetable oil

1 Place well-greased cast-iron corn stick pans in a 425° oven for 5 minutes or until hot.

2 Combine first 5 ingredients in a large bowl.

3 Combine eggs, milk, and oil; add to dry ingredients, stirring just until dry ingredients are moistened.

4 Spoon batter into hot pans, filling two-thirds full. Bake at 425° for 15 to 17 minutes or until corn sticks are golden. Yield: 14 corn sticks.

Orange-Glazed Tea Rolls

PREP: 18 MINUTES; BAKE: 11 MINUTES

1 (8-ounce) package refrigerated crescent dinner rolls
1 tablespoon butter or margarine, melted
⅓ cup sugar
¼ teaspoon ground cinnamon

Orange Glaze
Garnishes: cinnamon sticks, orange slices

1 Unroll crescent roll dough onto lightly floured wax paper; press perforations to seal. Brush dough with melted butter. Combine sugar and cinnamon; sprinkle over dough.

2 Roll up, jellyroll fashion, starting at long side, and cut into 1-inch slices. Place slices, cut sides down, in lightly greased miniature (1¾-inch) muffin pans. Bake at 375° for 11 to 13 minutes or until golden. Remove from pans immediately, and drizzle with Orange Glaze. Garnish, if desired. Yield: 1 dozen.

Orange Glaze

⅔ **cup sifted powdered sugar**
2 **tablespoons frozen orange juice**
   concentrate, thawed and
   undiluted
2 **teaspoons water**

1 Combine all ingredients, stirring until smooth. Yield: ¼ cup.

Orange-Glazed Tea Rolls (facing page)

Deep-Dish Cheesecake Coffee Cake

PREP: 20 MINUTES; BAKE: 40 MINUTES

3 cups biscuit and baking mix
½ cup milk
¼ cup sugar
¼ cup butter or margarine,
    melted

1 (8-ounce) package cream cheese,
    softened
2 large eggs
½ cup sugar
½ teaspoon vanilla extract

½ cup strawberry preserves
Garnish: strawberry fans

1 Combine first 4 ingredients; stir vigorously 30 seconds. Turn dough out onto a lightly floured surface; knead gently 4 or 5 times. Pat dough evenly into bottom and up sides of an ungreased 9-inch square pan.

2 Combine cream cheese and next 3 ingredients in a mixing bowl; beat with an electric mixer until smooth. Pour batter into pan, and bake at 350° for 40 to 45 minutes or until a wooden pick inserted in center comes out clean. Let stand 10 minutes.

3 Spread preserves over top; cut coffee cake into squares to serve. Garnish, if desired, and serve warm. Yield: 8 servings.

Toasted Rolls with Herb Butter

PREP: 9 MINUTES; BROIL: 2 MINUTES

Leftover hamburger buns are a fine substitute for the kaiser rolls in this recipe.

4 kaiser rolls
¼ cup butter or margarine,
    softened
2 tablespoons minced fresh
    parsley
1½ tablespoons minced fresh or
    freeze-dried chives
1½ teaspoons lemon juice

1 Slice rolls in half horizontally. Combine butter and remaining ingredients; spread evenly on cut sides of rolls.

2 Place roll halves, cut sides up, on a baking sheet; broil 5½ inches from heat (with electric oven door partially opened) 2 minutes or until toasted. Yield: 8 servings.

Cheesy French Bread

PREP: 5 MINUTES; COOK: 8 MINUTES

½ cup mayonnaise
¼ cup grated Parmesan cheese
1 clove garlic, minced

¼ cup (1 ounce) shredded
    Cheddar cheese
1½ teaspoons milk
¼ teaspoon paprika

1 (16-ounce) loaf unsliced French
    bread

1 Combine first 3 ingredients, and set aside.

2 Combine Cheddar cheese, milk, and paprika in a small saucepan; cook over low heat, stirring constantly, until cheese melts. Remove from heat; stir in mayonnaise mixture.

3 Slice bread loaf in half horizontally; place halves, cut sides up, on a large baking sheet. Broil 5½ inches from heat (with electric oven door partially opened) 2 minutes or until toasted. Spread toasted sides of bread halves with cheese mixture. Broil 5½ inches from heat (with electric oven door partially opened) 1 minute or until cheese mixture is lightly browned. Yield: 8 servings.

Parslied Garlic Bread

PREP: 7 MINUTES; GRILL: 15 MINUTES

¼ cup butter or margarine,
    softened
¼ cup chopped fresh parsley
1 clove garlic, crushed

1 (16-ounce) loaf sliced French
    bread

1 Combine first 3 ingredients.

2 Spread butter mixture between slices and on top of bread. Wrap loaf in heavy-duty aluminum foil. Grill, uncovered, over medium-hot coals (350° to 400°), about 15 minutes or until bread is thoroughly heated, turning often. Yield: 8 servings.

Feta Cheese Bread

PREP: 25 MINUTES; RISE: 45 MINUTES; BAKE: 35 MINUTES

FYI

Using rapid-rise yeast saves time because it is added directly to dry ingredients. Doughs made with rapid-rise yeast rise just once and take half the time to rise as doughs made with active dry yeast.

1½ cups milk
¼ cup water
¼ cup shortening

4 to 4½ cups all-purpose flour, divided
2 teaspoons sugar
½ teaspoon salt
1 package rapid-rise yeast

¼ cup butter or margarine, softened and divided
4 ounces feta cheese, crumbled and divided

2 tablespoons butter or margarine, melted

1 Combine first 3 ingredients in a saucepan; heat until shortening melts. Cool to 120° to 130°.

2 Combine 2 cups flour, sugar, salt, and yeast in a large mixing bowl. Add milk mixture, beating at low speed of an electric mixer. Beat 2 minutes at medium speed. Stir in enough remaining flour to make a soft dough. Turn dough out onto a floured surface; knead lightly 4 or 5 times. Divide dough in half.

3 Roll 1 portion of dough into a 16- x 8-inch rectangle; spread with half of softened butter, and sprinkle with half of cheese. Roll up dough, starting at long side; pinch ends to seal. Place dough, seam side down, in a well-greased French bread pan.

4 Repeat procedure with remaining dough, softened butter, and cheese. Brush each loaf with 1 tablespoon melted butter. Cover and let rise in a warm place (85°), free from drafts, 45 minutes or until doubled in bulk.

5 Bake, uncovered, at 375° for 15 minutes. Reduce temperature to 350°, and bake 20 minutes or until loaves sound hollow when tapped. Remove from pans immediately; cool on wire racks. Yield: 2 loaves.

Feta Cheese Bread (facing page)

Sour Cream Yeast Rolls

PREP: 15 MINUTES; RISE: 30 MINUTES; BAKE: 18 MINUTES

2 cups bread flour
¼ cup sugar
1½ teaspoons active dry yeast
½ teaspoon salt
¼ cup water
¼ cup sour cream
¼ cup butter or margarine, cut
    into small pieces
1 large egg

Melted butter or margarine
    (optional)

1 Combine first 8 ingredients in a 1-pound-loaf bread machine according to manufacturer's instructions. Process in dough cycle.

2 Turn dough out onto a heavily floured surface, and knead lightly 4 or 5 times. Divide dough in half. Shape each portion of dough into 9 balls, and place in a lightly greased 9-inch round pan. Cover and let rise in a warm place (85°), free from drafts, 30 minutes or until doubled in bulk.

3 Bake, uncovered, at 375° for 18 to 20 minutes or until golden. Brush hot rolls with melted butter, if desired. Yield: 1½ dozen.

FYI

Make sure the recipe you select for your bread machine is the right size for the machine. This recipe is designed for a bread machine that makes a one-pound loaf.

You don't have to slave over elaborate recipes with long ingredient lists to get a great-tasting dessert—just try these shortcut sweets. Our favorite recipe in this chapter, **FUDGE PIE**, with its ooey-gooey richness, will also top

DESSERTS

your family's list. And **EASY PECAN TARTS** and **BAKED APPLE TURNOVERS** will make great after-school snacks. For a quick-to-fix treat, keep one of our dessert sauces on hand to drizzle over ice cream or angel food cake. Take your pick—you'll find a recipe to satisfy that craving for a little something sweet, even when you're short on time.

Cherry Cordial Dessert (page 195), Brandy Peaches (page 191)

Easy Chocolate Chewies

PREP: 23 MINUTES; BAKE: 10 MINUTES

FYI

Store soft and chewy cookies like these in an airtight container so that they don't dry out. Keep crisp cookies in a jar with a loose-fitting lid. The small amount of circulating air will help to keep the cookies crisp.

½ cup shortening
1 (18.25-ounce) package devil's
   food cake mix
2 large eggs, lightly beaten
1 tablespoon water

½ cup sifted powdered sugar

1 Cut shortening into cake mix with a pastry blender until mixture is crumbly. Add eggs and water; stir until smooth. Let stand 5 minutes.

2 Shape dough into 1-inch balls. Roll balls in powdered sugar; place 2 inches apart on lightly greased cookie sheets. Bake at 375° for 10 minutes. Cool 1 minute on cookie sheets; remove to wire racks, and let cool completely. Yield: 4 dozen.

Peanut Butter Bars

PREP: 8 MINUTES; BAKE: 40 MINUTES

FYI

Chocolate may take on a chalky gray hue in warm places like kitchens. This discol- oration, or "bloom," indicates that cocoa butter has risen to the surface. Bloom doesn't affect the quality and disappears when the chocolate melts.

1 cup chunky peanut butter
½ cup butter or margarine,
   melted
2 large eggs
1 (18.25-ounce) package yellow
   cake mix

1 (6-ounce) package semisweet
   chocolate morsels
1 (14-ounce) can sweetened
   condensed milk

1 Combine first 4 ingredients in a large mixing bowl; beat at medium speed of an electric mixer 2 minutes.

2 Lightly grease sides of a 13- x 9- x 2-inch pan. Press half of cake mix mixture into prepared pan. Bake at 350° for 10 minutes; sprinkle with chocolate morsels. Drizzle sweet- ened condensed milk over mixture in pan; sprinkle with remaining cake mix mixture. Bake at 350° for 30 minutes. Cool in pan on a wire rack. Cut into squares. Yield: 2 dozen.

No-Bake Brownies

PREP: 6 MINUTES; COOK: 10 MINUTES; CHILL: 1 HOUR

1 (12-ounce) package semisweet
   chocolate morsels
1 cup plus 2 teaspoons evaporated
   milk, divided

1 (11-ounce) package vanilla
   wafers

2 cups miniature marshmallows
1 cup chopped pecans
1 cup sifted powdered sugar
½ teaspoon salt

1 Combine chocolate morsels and 1 cup evaporated milk in a saucepan; cook over low heat until chocolate melts, stirring occasionally. Set mixture aside.

2 Position knife blade in food processor bowl; add half of vanilla wafers. Process to make coarse crumbs. Place crumbs in a large bowl. Repeat procedure with remaining vanilla wafers.

3 Stir marshmallows and remaining 3 ingredients into crumbs. Reserve ½ cup chocolate mixture. Stir remaining chocolate mixture into crumb mixture. Press mixture evenly into a well-greased 9-inch square pan.

4 Combine reserved ½ cup chocolate mixture and remaining 2 teaspoons evaporated milk; spread evenly over crumb mixture. Cover and chill at least 1 hour. Cut into squares. Yield: 3 dozen.

FYI

These quick brownies cook on the stovetop just long enough to melt the chocolate. But that's it—there's no need to heat up the kitchen with the oven.

Chocolate-Rum Balls

PREP: 20 MINUTES

1 (9-ounce) package chocolate
    wafer cookies, crushed
1 cup finely chopped pecans
1 cup sifted powdered sugar
¼ cup dark rum
¼ cup light corn syrup

Additional sifted powdered sugar

1 Combine first 3 ingredients; stir in rum and corn syrup.

2 Shape mixture into 1-inch balls, and roll in additional powdered sugar. Store balls in an airtight container in refrigerator up to one month. Yield: 4 dozen.

Speedy Sweet Potato Pie

PREP: 7 MINUTES; BAKE: 50 MINUTES

1 (16-ounce) can cut sweet
    potatoes, drained and
    mashed
1 (14-ounce) can sweetened
    condensed milk
1 teaspoon vanilla extract
½ teaspoon ground nutmeg
2 large eggs

1 unbaked 9-inch pastry shell

1 Beat first 5 ingredients at medium speed of an electric mixer until well blended.

2 Pour filling into pastry shell. Bake at 425° for 15 minutes. Reduce oven temperature to 350°, and bake 35 additional minutes or until a knife inserted in center comes out clean. Yield: one 9-inch pie.

Chocolate-Cream Cheese Pie

PREP: 10 MINUTES; CHILL: 1 HOUR

FYI

Thaw an eight-ounce container of frozen whipped topping in the microwave, uncovered, at MEDIUM-LOW (30% power) for 1 to 1½ minutes.

1 (8-ounce) package cream
    cheese, softened
¾ cup sifted powdered sugar
¼ cup cocoa
1 (8-ounce) container frozen
    whipped topping, thawed

1 (6-ounce) chocolate-flavored
    crumb crust
½ cup chopped pecans, toasted

1 Beat cream cheese at high speed of an electric mixer until creamy. Add sugar and cocoa; beat well. Fold in whipped topping.

2 Spread mixture in crumb crust, and sprinkle with pecans. Chill at least 1 hour. Store in refrigerator. Yield: one 9-inch pie.

Fudge Pie

Fudge Pie

PREP: 10 MINUTES; BAKE: 35 MINUTES

3 large eggs, lightly beaten
1½ cups sugar
¾ cup chopped pecans
⅓ cup all-purpose flour
⅓ cup cocoa
¾ cup butter or margarine,
    melted
½ teaspoon vanilla extract

1 unbaked 9-inch pastry shell
Vanilla ice cream (optional)

1 Combine first 7 ingredients.

2 Pour mixture into pastry shell. Bake at 350° for 35 to 40 minutes or until set. Serve with ice cream, if desired. Yield: one 9-inch pie.

Creamy Dutch Apple Dessert

PREP: 10 MINUTES; BAKE: 18 MINUTES

FYI

You don't have to use a food processor to crush graham crackers. Use a rolling pin instead. Place the crackers in a heavy-duty, zip-top plastic bag, and seal. Then crush the crackers with the rolling pin.

1 cup graham cracker crumbs
3 tablespoons butter or margarine, melted

1 (14-ounce) can sweetened condensed milk
¼ cup lemon juice
1 (8-ounce) carton sour cream
1 (21-ounce) can apple pie filling

¼ cup chopped walnuts, toasted
½ teaspoon ground cinnamon

1 Combine cracker crumbs and butter; press mixture firmly into bottom of an 8-inch square baking dish.

2 Combine condensed milk and lemon juice; stir in sour cream. Spread mixture evenly over crust; top with pie filling. Bake at 400° for 18 minutes.

3 Combine walnuts and cinnamon; sprinkle over baked pie filling. Serve warm. Yield: 8 servings.

Easy Pecan Tarts

PREP: 10 MINUTES; BAKE: 16 MINUTES

FYI

Four ounces of shelled pecans equals the one cup of chopped pecans you'll need for this recipe.

2 large eggs, lightly beaten
1 cup chopped pecans
¾ cup firmly packed brown sugar
2 tablespoons butter or margarine, melted
1 teaspoon vanilla extract
Pinch of salt

8 (2-inch) unbaked tart shells
Garnishes: whipped cream, pecan halves

1 Combine first 6 ingredients.

2 Spoon pecan mixture into tart shells. Place filled shells on a baking sheet. Bake at 425° for 16 to 18 minutes or until filling is set. Cool completely on a wire rack. Garnish, if desired. Yield: 8 servings.

Baked Apple Turnovers

PREP: **29** MINUTES; BAKE: **13** MINUTES

1 cup apple pie filling
¼ teaspoon apple pie spice
  (optional)

1 (15-ounce) package refrigerated
  piecrusts

1 cup sifted powdered sugar
1 tablespoon plus 1 teaspoon milk
½ teaspoon vanilla extract

1 Chop pie filling. Stir apple pie spice into chopped pie filling, if desired. Set aside.

2 Unfold piecrusts, pressing lightly to remove fold lines; cut into 8 (4½-inch) circles. For each turnover, spoon 2 tablespoons pie filling mixture onto half of pastry circle. Moisten edges of circle with water; fold dough over filling, pressing edges to seal. Crimp edges with a fork. Place turnovers on a lightly greased baking sheet. Bake at 425° for 13 to 15 minutes or until golden.

3 Combine powdered sugar, milk, and vanilla, stirring until smooth. Drizzle glaze over warm turnovers. Yield: 8 turnovers.

Baked Apple Turnovers

Almond-Raspberry Brie

Almond-Raspberry Brie

PREP: 10 MINUTES; MICROWAVE: 1 ½ MINUTES

FYI

Keep Brie tightly wrapped until ready to use. The snowy white rind is edible, so you don't need to remove it before serving the cheese.

1 (15-ounce) round Brie

2 tablespoons seedless red raspberry jam

1 tablespoon Chambord or other raspberry-flavored liqueur (optional)

3 tablespoons sliced almonds, toasted

1½ teaspoons brown sugar

1 tablespoon honey

1 Remove rind from top of cheese, cutting to within ½ inch of outside edges. Place cheese on a microwave-safe plate.

2 Combine jam and, if desired, liqueur; stir well with a wire whisk. Spread mixture over top of cheese. Sprinkle almonds and brown sugar evenly over jam mixture; drizzle with honey.

3 Microwave at HIGH 1½ minutes or just until cheese is softened. Serve Brie immediately with gingersnaps. Yield: 8 servings.

Orange-Glazed Bananas Foster

PREP: 10 MINUTES; BAKE: 15 MINUTES

4 bananas, split lengthwise and
 quartered
¾ cup orange juice
¼ cup Grand Marnier or other
 orange-flavored liqueur
2 tablespoons butter or margarine

⅓ cup chopped walnuts
⅓ cup firmly packed brown sugar
Vanilla ice cream

1 Arrange banana quarters in an 8-inch square baking dish. Combine orange juice and liqueur; pour over banana. Dot with butter. Bake at 400° for 10 minutes, basting once with orange juice mixture.

2 Combine walnuts and brown sugar; sprinkle over banana mixture. Bake 5 additional minutes. Serve immediately over ice cream. Yield: 8 servings.

Brandy Peaches

PREP: 7 MINUTES; BAKE: 20 MINUTES

2 (16-ounce) cans peach halves in
 juice

½ cup firmly packed brown sugar
½ cup maple syrup
3 tablespoons butter or
 margarine, melted
Ground cinnamon
3 tablespoons brandy

Vanilla ice cream

1 Place 8 peach halves, cavity sides up, in a lightly greased 8-inch square baking dish; reserve remaining peaches and juice for another use.

2 Spoon sugar, syrup, and butter evenly over peaches; sprinkle with cinnamon. Bake, uncovered, at 325° for 20 minutes. Remove from oven; sprinkle brandy over peaches.

3 Place each peach half in an individual serving dish, and top with a scoop of ice cream. Spoon sauce from baking dish over ice cream. Yield: 8 servings.

Easy Strawberry Trifle

PREP: 17 MINUTES

FYI

Wash strawberries just before using them, and hull them after washing so they don't become mushy.

1 (7-ounce) package jellyrolls

1 (3½-ounce) package vanilla instant pudding mix
1½ cups milk
3 cups frozen whipped topping, thawed and divided

2 cups sliced fresh strawberries
Garnish: whole strawberries

1 Cut each jellyroll crosswise into 3 slices; arrange slices, cut sides down, on bottom and around sides of a 2½-quart soufflé or trifle dish. Fill in with remaining jellyroll slices.

2 Prepare pudding mix according to package directions, using 1½ cups milk; let stand 5 minutes. Fold in 1 cup whipped topping.

3 Arrange half of sliced strawberries over jellyroll slices; top with pudding mixture. Arrange remaining sliced strawberries over pudding mixture; dollop or pipe remaining 2 cups whipped topping over pudding mixture. Garnish, if desired. Yield: about 8 servings.

Elegant Fresh Fruit

PREP: 14 MINUTES

FYI

Purchase fresh pineapple already peeled and cored to make this recipe even quicker. Dip the peaches into boiling water for 30 seconds before you peel them. The skins will then slip off easily.

1 (8-ounce) package cream cheese, softened
1 (7-ounce) jar marshmallow creme

3 cups sliced fresh peaches
3 cups seedless red grapes (about 1¼ pounds)
2 cups fresh blueberries
1 peeled and cored fresh pineapple, cut into 1-inch pieces
⅓ cup cognac

1 Beat cream cheese at high speed of an electric mixer until creamy. Add marshmallow creme, and beat well. Set aside.

2 Combine peaches and remaining 4 ingredients in a large bowl. Serve fruit mixture with cream cheese mixture. Yield: 8 servings.

Apricot Ice Cream Sauce

PREP: 5 MINUTES

1 (12-ounce) jar apricot preserves
⅓ cup firmly packed brown sugar
⅓ cup unsweetened pineapple
   juice
1½ tablespoons grated orange or
   lemon rind

1 Combine all ingredients; stir until sugar dissolves. Serve over vanilla ice cream. Yield: 1⅔ cups.

Apricot Ice Cream Sauce (above), Fresh Plum Sauce (page 194)

Fresh Plum Sauce

PREP: 5 MINUTES; COOK: 15 MINUTES; CHILL: 1 HOUR

1 pound ripe plums, pitted and
    quartered (about 4 plums)
½ cup water
¼ cup sugar
¼ teaspoon ground cinnamon

3 tablespoons port or other sweet
    red wine

1 Combine first 4 ingredients in a small saucepan. Bring to a boil; reduce heat, and simmer 15 minutes or until plums are soft.

2 Pour mixture through a wire-mesh strainer into a small bowl, pressing mixture against sides of strainer with back of spoon; discard solids. Cool liquid mixture slightly; stir in port. Cover and chill at least 1 hour. Serve over vanilla ice cream. Yield: 1¼ cups.

Rum Sundae Sauce

PREP: 3 MINUTES; COOK: 7 MINUTES

Store brown sugar in an airtight container or zip-top plastic bag to keep it from drying.
If the brown sugar does harden, place an apple wedge in the container with the sugar; remove the wedge once the sugar softens.

¾ cup firmly packed brown sugar
⅓ cup water
⅓ cup light corn syrup
2 tablespoons butter or margarine
⅛ teaspoon salt

½ teaspoon rum extract

1 Combine first 5 ingredients in a medium saucepan; cook over medium heat, stirring until sugar dissolves. Reduce heat to low; cook, without stirring, until a candy thermometer registers 230° (about 5 minutes). Remove from heat, and cool slightly.

2 Stir in rum extract. Serve warm over ice cream. Yield: 1 cup.

Note: Refrigerate Rum Sundae Sauce up to 2 weeks.

Toffee Sauce

PREP: 5 MINUTES; COOK: 8 MINUTES

½ cup sugar
½ cup whipping cream
¼ cup light corn syrup
2 tablespoons butter or margarine

5 (1.4-ounce) butter toffee-
    flavored candy bars,
    chopped

1 Combine first 4 ingredients in a large saucepan. Cook over medium heat, stirring constantly, until mixture comes to a boil; boil 2 minutes.

2 Remove saucepan from heat; stir in chopped candy. Serve with fresh fruit or ice cream. Yield: 2 cups.

Cherry Cordial Dessert

PREP: 18 MINUTES; FREEZE: 4 HOURS

½ gallon vanilla ice cream,
    softened
1 cup maraschino cherries, halved
½ cup coarsely chopped pecans
4 (1.55-ounce) milk chocolate
    bars, finely chopped

¼ cup crème de cacao
Garnishes: sweetened whipped
    cream, maraschino cherries

1 Combine first 4 ingredients; spoon mixture into a 9-inch springform pan. Cover and freeze at least 4 hours or until firm.

2 Carefully remove sides of springform pan. Cut into wedges to serve. Spoon crème de cacao over each serving. Garnish, if desired. Serve immediately. Yield: 8 servings.

FYI

Soften ice cream by microwaving it at MEDIUM (50% power) for 30 seconds or until soft.

Double Delight Ice Cream Pie

PREP: 6 MINUTES; FREEZE: 5 HOURS

2 cups butter pecan ice cream,
    softened
1 (9-inch) graham cracker crust
2 (1.4-ounce) English toffee-
    flavored candy bars, crushed

2 cups vanilla ice cream, softened

1 Spread butter pecan ice cream in crust; sprinkle with half of crushed candy bars. Cover; freeze 1 hour.

2 Spread vanilla ice cream over top; sprinkle with remaining crushed candy bars. Cover; freeze 4 hours or until firm. Yield: one 9-inch pie.

FYI

Crush the candy bars for this recipe in the food processor using the knife blade.

Sunshine Fizz

Sunshine Fizz

PREP: 5 MINUTES

1 cup orange juice, chilled
1 cup pineapple juice, chilled
1 cup orange sherbet

½ cup club soda, chilled
Additional orange sherbet
Garnishes: pineapple wedges,
    maraschino cherries

1 Combine first 3 ingredients in container of an electric blender; cover and process until smooth, stopping once to scrape down sides.

2 Stir club soda into juice mixture, and pour into tall glasses. Add a scoop of orange sherbet to each glass. Garnish, if desired. Serve immediately. Yield: 3 cups.

Brandy Alexander

PREP: 7 MINUTES

1 quart vanilla ice cream
¼ cup brandy
¼ cup crème de cacao

1 Combine all ingredients in container of an electric blender; cover and process until smooth, stopping once to scrape down sides. Serve immediately. Yield: 3 cups.

Mocha Frosty

PREP: 10 MINUTES

¼ cup milk
2 teaspoons instant coffee granules

3 cups vanilla ice cream
⅓ cup fudge sauce

1 Combine milk and coffee granules; stir until coffee is dissolved.

2 Combine coffee mixture, ice cream, and fudge sauce in container of an electric blender; cover and process until smooth, stopping once to scrape down sides. Serve immediately. Yield: about 3 cups.

Kahlúa Velvet Frosty

PREP: 5 MINUTES

1 pint vanilla ice cream
1 cup Kahlúa or other coffee-flavored liqueur
1 cup half-and-half
⅛ teaspoon almond extract
Ice cubes

1 Combine first 4 ingredients in container of an electric blender. Add enough ice cubes to measure 5 cups in blender. Cover and process until smooth, stopping once to scrape down sides. Serve immediately. Yield: 5 cups.

FYI

Make this beverage before dinner, and place the blender container with the prepared mixture in the freezer until serving time.

Caramel Toffee Bombe (page 221)

Ready
WHEN YOU ARE

Wish you had time to prepare an elegant dinner for company or something special for a weeknight supper? You will with these make-ahead ideas. We've included all types of recipes, from taste-tempting appetizers like

MAKE IT AHEAD

TEXAS CAVIAR to frosty desserts like **COOKIES AND CREAM CRUNCH** (with entrées, salads, soups, and breads in between). Just prepare them at your leisure, and then store them according to the recipe directions by freezing, marinating, or chilling. All you'll have left to do is thaw and cook, or—better yet—just stir and serve.

Clockwise from bottom: Grilled Pork Tenderloin (page 210), Asparagus Vinaigrette (page 216), Spoon Rolls (page 218)

Texas Caviar

PREP: 20 MINUTES; CHILL: 2 HOURS

FYI

Chop fresh parsley quickly by placing it in a measuring cup and snipping it with kitchen shears.

2 (14-ounce) cans black-eyed peas, drained
1 (15½-ounce) can hominy, drained
½ cup chopped onion
½ cup chopped fresh parsley
4 green onions, thinly sliced
2 medium tomatoes, chopped
2 cloves garlic, minced
1 medium-size green pepper, seeded and chopped
1 jalapeño pepper, seeded and chopped
1 (8-ounce) bottle Italian salad dressing

1 Combine all ingredients in a large bowl; cover and chill at least 2 hours. Drain before serving. Serve with tortilla chips. Yield: 8 cups.

Chutney and Blue Cheese Ball

PREP: 10 MINUTES; CHILL: 3 HOURS

1 (8-ounce) package cream cheese, softened
1 (4-ounce) package crumbled blue cheese
¼ cup chutney

¾ cup chopped almonds, toasted

1 Combine first 3 ingredients; cover and chill 1 hour.

2 Shape cheese mixture into a ball; roll in almonds. Cover and chill at least 2 hours. Serve with crackers. Yield: one 4½-inch cheese ball.

202 Make It Ahead

Marinated Mushrooms

PREP: 8 MINUTES; MARINATE: 8 HOURS

1 (2-ounce) can anchovies,
    drained and mashed
1 (2-ounce) jar diced pimiento,
    drained
1⅓ cups vegetable oil
1 cup lemon juice
½ teaspoon dried tarragon
½ teaspoon dried basil
¼ teaspoon dried oregano
⅛ teaspoon pepper
1 clove garlic, minced

2 pounds small fresh mushrooms

Lettuce leaves (optional)

1 Combine first 9 ingredients, stirring well with a wire whisk. Pour mixture into a large heavy-duty, zip-top plastic bag.

2 Add mushrooms to bag; seal bag. Shake gently to coat mushrooms. Marinate in refrigerator 8 hours, turning bag occasionally.

3 Drain mushroom mixture, discarding marinade. Serve mushrooms in a lettuce-lined bowl, if desired. Yield: 20 appetizer servings.

FYI

Clean mushrooms by wiping them with a damp paper towel. Rinsing mushrooms in water makes them soggy.

Freezer Pizza Snacks

PREP: 11 MINUTES; FREEZE: 1 HOUR; BAKE: 15 MINUTES

½ cup (2 ounces) shredded sharp
    Cheddar cheese
½ cup (2 ounces) shredded
    part-skim mozzarella cheese
⅓ cup chopped pepperoni
⅓ cup mayonnaise
¼ cup chopped onion
3 tablespoons chopped ripe olives
1 (2½-ounce) jar sliced
    mushrooms, drained

5 English muffins, split

1 Combine first 7 ingredients.

2 Spread cheese mixture evenly over muffin halves, and place on baking sheets. Freeze pizzas, uncovered, 1 hour or until frozen. Remove frozen pizzas from baking sheets, and place in an airtight container. Freeze up to 1 month.

3 To serve, place frozen pizzas on ungreased baking sheets. Bake at 350° for 15 minutes or until thoroughly heated and lightly browned. Yield: 10 servings.

Antipasto Kabobs

PREP: 15 MINUTES; COOK: 10 MINUTES; MARINATE: 4 HOURS

½ (9-ounce) package refrigerated
    cheese-filled tortellini

1 (14-ounce) can artichoke hearts,
    drained and quartered
1 (6-ounce) can large pitted ripe
    olives, drained
½ (8-ounce) package sliced
    pepperoni
1 (8-ounce) bottle reduced-fat
    Parmesan Italian salad
    dressing

Garnish: fresh oregano sprig

1 Cook tortellini according to package directions. Drain and cool.

2 Thread tortellini, artichoke hearts, olives, and pepperoni slices onto 24 (6-inch) wooden skewers. Place kabobs in a 13- x 9- x 2-inch dish; drizzle with salad dressing, turning to coat. Cover and marinate in refrigerator at least 4 hours, turning kabobs occasionally.

3 Remove kabobs from marinade; discard marinade. Arrange kabobs on a serving platter, and garnish, if desired. Yield: 12 appetizer servings.

Antipasto Kabobs

Piña Colada Slush

PREP: 3 MINUTES; FREEZE: 8 HOURS

3 cups water, divided
1 (15-ounce) can cream of
    coconut
1 (46-ounce) can pineapple juice
2 (12-ounce) cans frozen
    lemonade concentrate,
    thawed and undiluted
2 to 3 cups light rum

1 (3-liter) bottle lemon-lime
    carbonated beverage, chilled

1 Combine 1 cup water and cream of coconut in a large plastic container, stirring until smooth. Add remaining 2 cups water, pineapple juice, lemonade concentrate, and rum, stirring until blended. Cover and freeze at least 8 hours, stirring twice.

2 To serve, combine equal amounts frozen mixture and lemon-lime beverage, stirring well. Serve immediately. Store any remaining frozen mixture in freezer. Yield: 6 quarts.

Punch for a Bunch

PREP: 3 MINUTES; COOK: 15 MINUTES; FREEZE: 8 HOURS

8 cups water, divided
1½ cups sugar

1 (7½-ounce) bottle frozen lemon
    juice, thawed
1 (6-ounce) can frozen orange
    juice concentrate
2 (6-ounce) cans unsweetened
    pineapple juice, chilled

1 (2-liter) bottle ginger ale,
    chilled

1 Combine 2 cups water and sugar in a large saucepan. Bring to a boil; reduce heat, and simmer, uncovered, 15 minutes.

2 Remove saucepan from heat; stir in remaining 6 cups water, lemon juice, frozen orange juice concentrate, and pineapple juice. Pour mixture into a 13- x 9- x 2-inch dish; cover and freeze at least 8 hours, stirring twice.

3 To serve, let frozen mixture stand at room temperature at least 30 minutes or until mixture can be broken into chunks. Spoon chunks into a punch bowl; add ginger ale, and stir gently until slushy. Yield: 5 quarts.

FYI

Planning a party, shower, or wedding reception? This is a perfect make-ahead bonus. Prepare steps 1 and 2 of Punch for a Bunch, and freeze for up to 3 months.

Shrimp with Green Peppercorn Sauce

Shrimp with Green Peppercorn Sauce

PREP: 10 MINUTES; CHILL: 1 HOUR; COOK: 3 MINUTES

1 cup mayonnaise or salad
   dressing
2 tablespoons Dijon mustard
2 cloves garlic, pressed
1 (3-ounce) jar green peppercorns
   in liquid, drained

4½ cups water
1 teaspoon liquid shrimp-and-crab
   boil seasoning
1½ pounds unpeeled medium-size
   fresh shrimp
Garnish: fresh rosemary sprigs

1 Combine first 4 ingredients in container of an electric blender; cover and process until smooth, stopping once to scrape down sides. Transfer to a small bowl; cover and chill at least 1 hour.

2 Combine water and shrimp-and-crab boil seasoning in a Dutch oven; bring to a boil. Add shrimp, and cook 3 to 5 minutes or until shrimp turn pink. Drain well. Arrange shrimp on a serving platter; garnish, if desired. Serve with chilled sauce. Yield: 4 servings.

Filet Mignon Tarragon

PREP: 5 MINUTES; MARINATE: 3 HOURS; BROIL: 14 MINUTES

2 (4-ounce) beef tenderloin
    steaks, trimmed
¼ cup dry red wine
2 tablespoons soy sauce
¾ teaspoon fresh tarragon or
    ¼ teaspoon dried tarragon

Vegetable cooking spray
Garnish: fresh tarragon sprigs

1 Place steaks in a heavy-duty, zip-top plastic bag. Combine wine, soy sauce, and ¾ teaspoon fresh tarragon; pour over steaks. Seal bag; marinate in refrigerator 3 hours, turning bag occasionally.

2 Remove steaks from marinade; discard marinade. Place steaks on a rack coated with cooking spray; place rack in a broiler pan. Broil 5½ inches from heat (with electric oven door partially opened) 7 to 9 minutes on each side or to desired degree of doneness. Garnish, if desired. Yield: 2 servings.

Line the broiler pan with aluminum foil for easy cleanup.

Flank Steak Pinwheels

PREP: 10 MINUTES; MARINATE: 8 HOURS; GRILL: 8 MINUTES

2 (1-pound) flank steaks
1 large onion, chopped

1 cup vegetable oil
⅔ cup red wine vinegar
2 teaspoons salt
1½ teaspoons fresh thyme or
    ½ teaspoon dried thyme
1½ teaspoons fresh marjoram or
    ½ teaspoon dried marjoram
Dash of pepper
4 cloves garlic, minced

Garnish: fresh thyme or marjoram
    sprigs

1 Slice steaks diagonally across grain into ½-inch-wide strips; roll up strips, and secure with wooden picks. Place pinwheels in a 13- x 9- x 2-inch dish; sprinkle with onion.

2 Combine oil and next 6 ingredients; pour over pinwheels. Cover and marinate in refrigerator 8 hours, turning occasionally.

3 Remove pinwheels from marinade; discard marinade. Grill, covered, over medium-hot coals (350° to 400°) 4 to 5 minutes on each side or to desired degree of doneness. Garnish, if desired. Yield: 8 servings.

Most supermarkets carry minced garlic in a jar; it's quicker and easier than mincing fresh garlic. Look for it in the produce section.

Spaghetti Casserole

PREP: 12 MINUTES; CHILL: UP TO 24 HOURS; BAKE: 1 HOUR

FYI

*Preparing a big batch
of chopped onion or
peppers to keep on
hand is easy. Spread
the chopped vegetables
in a thin layer on a
baking sheet; freeze 30
minutes. Crumble and
freeze in a zip-top
freezer bag up to one
month.*

½ (16-ounce) package thin
    spaghetti

1 pound ground chuck
1 large onion, chopped
1 small green pepper, seeded and
    chopped

1 (10¾-ounce) can tomato soup,
    undiluted
1 (8-ounce) can whole kernel
    corn, drained
2 cups (8 ounces) shredded
    Cheddar cheese
⅔ cup water
½ cup sliced pimiento-stuffed
    olives
1½ teaspoons dried Italian
    seasoning
½ teaspoon salt

1 Cook pasta according to package directions; drain.

2 While pasta cooks, cook ground chuck, onion, and green pepper in a Dutch oven over medium-high heat until meat is browned, stirring until meat crumbles; drain.

3 Stir soup and remaining 6 ingredients into meat mixture. Stir in cooked pasta. Spoon mixture into a lightly greased 13- x 9- x 2-inch baking dish. Cover and chill up to 24 hours.

4 Bake casserole, covered, at 350° for 1 hour or until mixture is thoroughly heated. Yield: 8 servings.

Note: To freeze Spaghetti Casserole, prepare as directed above, but do not bake. Cover tightly, and freeze up to 2 months. Thaw in refrigerator 24 hours. Bake as directed above.

Potato Breakfast Casserole

PREP: 15 MINUTES; CHILL: 8 HOURS; BAKE: 35 MINUTES

1 quart hot water
1 (6-ounce) package hash brown
   potato mix

5 large eggs, lightly beaten
1 cup (4 ounces) shredded Swiss
   cheese
½ cup small-curd cottage cheese
1 teaspoon salt
⅛ teaspoon pepper
⅛ teaspoon hot sauce
1 green onion, chopped
6 slices bacon, cooked, drained,
   and crumbled
Paprika

Garnish: fresh whole strawberries

1 Pour water over hash brown mix; let stand 10 minutes. Drain well.

2 Combine eggs and next 6 ingredients. Add hash brown mix, stirring well. Pour mixture into a buttered 10-inch pieplate. Sprinkle with bacon and paprika. Cover and chill 8 hours.

3 Bake, uncovered, at 350° for 35 minutes or until mixture is set. Cut into wedges to serve. Garnish, if desired. Yield: 6 servings.

Potato Breakfast Casserole

Grilled Pork Tenderloin

PREP: 5 MINUTES; MARINATE: 8 HOURS; GRILL: 15 MINUTES

Cutting meat to see if it's done lets the juices run out. Instead, use a meat thermometer.

2 (¾-pound) pork tenderloins
½ cup dry sherry or orange juice
½ cup soy sauce
2 tablespoons brown sugar
1 teaspoon ground ginger
2 cloves garlic, pressed

1 Place tenderloins in a heavy-duty, zip-top plastic bag. Combine sherry and remaining 4 ingredients; pour over tenderloins. Seal bag; marinate in refrigerator 8 hours, turning bag occasionally.

2 Remove tenderloins from marinade, discarding marinade. Grill, covered, over medium-hot coals (350° to 400°) 15 minutes or until a meat thermometer inserted in thickest portion of 1 tenderloin registers 160°, turning once. Cut into slices to serve. Yield: 6 servings.

Easy Grilled Ham

PREP: 6 MINUTES; MARINATE: 8 HOURS; GRILL: 30 MINUTES

1 (2-inch-thick) boneless fully
    cooked ham steak
½ cup ginger ale
½ cup orange juice
¼ cup firmly packed brown sugar
1 tablespoon vegetable oil
1½ teaspoons white vinegar
1 teaspoon dry mustard
¼ teaspoon ground ginger
⅛ teaspoon ground cloves

1 Place ham in a large shallow dish or heavy-duty, zip-top plastic bag. Combine ginger ale and remaining 7 ingredients; pour over ham. Cover dish, or seal bag; marinate in refrigerator 8 hours, turning occasionally.

2 Remove ham from marinade, discarding marinade. Grill ham, covered, over medium-hot coals (350° to 400°) 15 minutes on each side or until meat thermometer registers 140°. Yield: 10 servings.

Swiss Chicken Casserole

PREP: 6 MINUTES; CHILL: UP TO 24 HOURS; BAKE: 65 MINUTES

6 skinned and boned chicken
  breast halves
6 (4- x 4-inch) slices Swiss cheese
1 (10¾-ounce) can cream of
  chicken soup, undiluted
¼ cup milk
2 cups herb-seasoned stuffing mix
¼ cup butter or margarine,
  melted

1 Arrange chicken in an 11- x 7- x 1½-inch baking dish. Top each chicken breast half with a cheese slice. Combine soup and milk; spoon over chicken. Sprinkle with stuffing mix, and drizzle with butter. Cover and chill up to 24 hours.

2 Bake, covered, at 350° for 55 minutes. Uncover casserole, and bake 10 additional minutes or until thoroughly heated. Yield: 6 servings.

To freeze, prepare the casserole as directed, but don't bake. Cover and freeze up to two months. Thaw in refrigerator 24 hours. Bake as directed for 1 hour and 15 minutes or until thoroughly heated.

Chicken-Wild Rice Casserole

PREP: 8 MINUTES; CHILL: 8 HOURS; COOK: 1 HOUR

1 (6-ounce) package long-grain-
  and-wild rice mix

¼ cup butter or margarine
¼ cup all-purpose flour
1 (12-ounce) can evaporated milk
½ cup chicken broth
¼ teaspoon salt

2½ cups chopped cooked chicken
⅓ cup chopped green pepper
¼ cup chopped pimiento
1 (3-ounce) can sliced
  mushrooms, drained
¼ cup slivered almonds, toasted

1 Prepare rice mix according to package directions.

2 While rice cooks, melt butter in a saucepan over low heat; add flour, stirring until smooth. Cook, stirring constantly, 1 minute. Gradually add milk and broth; cook over medium heat, stirring constantly, until thickened and bubbly. Stir in salt.

3 Combine rice, sauce mixture, chicken, and next 3 ingredients; pour into a lightly greased 2-quart baking dish. Sprinkle with almonds. Cover and chill at least 8 hours and up to 24 hours.

4 Bake, uncovered, at 350° for 35 minutes or until thoroughly heated. Yield: 6 servings.

This casserole is perfect for weeknight entertaining. You can have it on the table 35 minutes after you get home from work because you'll have already done the prep work.

Fresh Fruit Soup

PREP: **25** MINUTES; COOK: **5** MINUTES; CHILL: UP TO **24** HOURS

2 tablespoons cornstarch
1 cup cold water, divided
¾ cup dry white wine
¾ cup maple-flavored syrup
1 teaspoon lemon juice

2 cups coarsely chopped fresh peaches
1 cup sliced fresh strawberries
1 cup fresh blueberries

1 Combine cornstarch and ¼ cup water in a large saucepan; stir until smooth. Stir in remaining ¾ cup water, wine, syrup, and lemon juice. Cook over medium heat, stirring constantly, until mixture comes to a boil; boil 1 minute. Remove pan from heat.

2 Place pan in a bowl of ice; stir often until mixture is completely cool. Stir in fruit. Cover and chill up to 24 hours. Yield: 5 cups.

Cold Cucumber Soup

PREP: **12** MINUTES; CHILL: UP TO **24** HOURS

3 medium cucumbers, peeled, seeded, and coarsely chopped
2 green onions, sliced
1 tablespoon lemon juice
1 tablespoon Worcestershire sauce
½ teaspoon celery salt
½ teaspoon dried dillweed
¼ teaspoon pepper

1½ cups sour cream

1 Combine first 7 ingredients in container of an electric blender; cover and process until smooth.

2 Whisk sour cream into cucumber mixture. Cover and chill up to 24 hours. Yield: 3½ cups.

Gazpacho

PREP: 10 MINUTES; CHILL: 8 HOURS

1½ cups tomato juice
1¼ cups water
¾ cup chopped cucumber
¾ cup chopped tomato
½ cup chopped green pepper
½ cup chopped onion
2 tablespoons red wine vinegar
1 tablespoon lemon juice
¼ teaspoon pepper
¼ teaspoon hot sauce
1 (10¾-ounce) can tomato soup,
    undiluted
1 clove garlic, minced

1 Combine all ingredients in a large bowl; cover and chill at least 8 hours. Yield: about 6 cups.

Frozen Fruit Salad

PREP: 10 MINUTES; FREEZE: 8 HOURS

½ cup chopped pecans, toasted
1 (16½-ounce) can pitted dark
    sweet cherries, drained
1 (15¼-ounce) can pineapple
    chunks, drained

1 (12-ounce) container frozen
    whipped topping, thawed
1 (8-ounce) carton lemon yogurt
½ cup mayonnaise

Green leaf lettuce (optional)

1 Combine first 3 ingredients in a large bowl.

2 Combine whipped topping, yogurt, and mayonnaise, stirring gently; fold into fruit mixture. Spoon mixture into an 11- x 7- x 1½-inch dish; cover and freeze at least 8 hours or until firm.

3 Cut frozen salad into squares, and serve on lettuce leaves, if desired. Yield: 8 servings.

Hearts of Palm Salad

Hearts of Palm Salad

PREP: 16 MINUTES; CHILL: 8 HOURS

½ cup olive oil
½ cup white wine vinegar
½ cup finely chopped celery
¼ cup finely chopped sweet red pepper
¼ cup finely chopped onion
¼ cup finely chopped dill pickle
2 tablespoons chopped ripe olives
1 teaspoon sugar
2 cloves garlic, pressed

6 cups torn romaine lettuce
1 (16-ounce) can hearts of palm, drained and cut into ½-inch pieces

1 Combine first 9 ingredients; cover and chill at least 8 hours, stirring occasionally.

2 To serve, arrange lettuce on 6 salad plates; top evenly with hearts of palm. Spoon vegetable mixture evenly over salads. Yield: 6 servings.

West Indies Salad

PREP: 10 MINUTES; CHILL: 4 HOURS

½ cup cider vinegar
½ cup vegetable oil
½ cup ice water
1 medium onion, finely chopped
1 pound fresh lump crabmeat,
　　drained

Red leaf lettuce
Garnish: tomato wedges

1 Combine first 4 ingredients in a medium nonmetal bowl; stir with a wire whisk until blended. Add crabmeat, and toss gently. Cover and chill 4 hours.

2 To serve, arrange lettuce leaves on individual serving plates. Drain crabmeat mixture, and spoon onto lettuce leaves. Garnish, if desired. Yield: 4 servings.

Layered Ham-Blue Cheese Salad

PREP: 20 MINUTES; CHILL: 3 HOURS

1 (8-ounce) package cream cheese,
　　softened
¾ cup crumbled blue cheese
⅓ cup milk
¼ cup mayonnaise or salad
　　dressing
1 tablespoon chopped fresh chives
2 teaspoons lemon juice

8 cups torn mixed salad greens
3 cups chopped cooked ham
2 cups chopped tomato
1 cup shredded carrot
½ cup chopped green pepper

1 cup croutons

1 Combine first 6 ingredients in a mixing bowl; beat at low speed of an electric mixer until smooth.

2 Layer half each of salad greens, ham, tomato, carrot, and green pepper in a large salad bowl. Spread half of blue cheese mixture over salad. Repeat layering procedure with remaining salad greens, ham, tomato, carrot, and green pepper. Spread remaining blue cheese mixture over top of salad. Cover and chill at least 3 hours.

3 Just before serving, sprinkle salad with croutons. Yield: 8 servings.

FYI

Purchase washed and torn mixed salad greens in the produce department of your supermarket.

Asparagus Vinaigrette

PREP: 8 MINUTES; COOK: 10 MINUTES; MARINATE: 8 HOURS

FYI

Squeeze a piece of onion through a garlic press to grate a small amount of onion easily.

3 pounds fresh asparagus spears

1 sweet red pepper, seeded and cut into strips
½ cup vegetable oil, divided

¼ cup white wine vinegar
2 tablespoons water
1 tablespoon grated onion
1 teaspoon dry mustard
½ teaspoon salt
Pinch of pepper

1 Snap off tough ends of asparagus. Remove scales from stalks with a knife or vegetable peeler, if desired. Arrange asparagus in a steamer basket over boiling water. Cover and steam 4 to 6 minutes or until crisp-tender. Plunge into ice water; drain.

2 Cook red pepper strips in 1 tablespoon hot oil in a medium skillet over medium-high heat, stirring constantly, until crisp-tender. Plunge into ice water; drain.

3 Place asparagus spears and pepper strips in a large shallow dish. Combine remaining oil, wine vinegar, and remaining 5 ingredients; pour over vegetables. Cover and chill at least 8 hours. Drain before serving. Yield: 12 servings.

Basil-Marinated Tomatoes

PREP: 10 MINUTES; MARINATE: 8 HOURS

3 large tomatoes

⅓ cup olive oil
¼ cup red wine vinegar
2 tablespoons chopped fresh basil
2 tablespoons chopped onion
1 teaspoon salt
¼ teaspoon pepper
1 clove garlic, pressed

1 Cut tomatoes into ½-inch-thick slices; arrange in a thin layer in a large shallow dish.

2 Combine oil and remaining 6 ingredients in a jar; cover tightly, and shake vigorously. Pour mixture over tomato slices. Cover and marinate in refrigerator at least 8 hours. Yield: 6 servings.

Marinated Zucchini

PREP: 13 MINUTES; MARINATE: 8 HOURS

3 medium zucchini, thinly sliced
  (about 1¼ pounds)
¼ cup chopped onion
¼ cup chopped green pepper
¼ cup chopped celery
1 tablespoon chopped pimiento

⅓ cup cider vinegar
¼ cup sugar
¼ cup vegetable oil
1 tablespoon white wine vinegar
½ teaspoon salt
¼ teaspoon pepper
⅛ teaspoon hot sauce

1 Combine first 5 ingredients in a large bowl; toss lightly.

2 Combine cider vinegar and remaining 6 ingredients; pour over zucchini mixture. Cover and marinate in refrigerator at least 8 hours, stirring occasionally. Serve with a slotted spoon. Yield: 4 servings.

Grilled Vegetable Kabobs

PREP: 11 MINUTES; MARINATE: 8 HOURS; GRILL: 10 MINUTES

4 medium-size sweet red peppers,
  seeded and cut into ½-inch
  strips
4 small zucchini, cut into ½-inch-
  thick slices

½ cup vegetable oil
¼ cup lemon juice
¼ cup white wine vinegar
1 tablespoon plus 1 teaspoon
  Worcestershire sauce
2 teaspoons dried Italian
  seasoning
1 teaspoon salt

1 Thread pepper strips and zucchini slices onto 8 (6-inch) bamboo skewers. Place kabobs in a shallow dish.

2 Combine oil and remaining 5 ingredients; pour over kabobs. Cover and marinate in refrigerator 8 hours, turning once.

3 Remove kabobs from marinade, reserving marinade. Grill kabobs, covered, over medium-hot coals (350° to 400°) 10 to 12 minutes or until vegetables are crisp-tender, turning and brushing with marinade occasionally. Yield: 4 servings.

Refrigerator Bran Muffins

PREP: 10 MINUTES; CHILL: 8 HOURS; BAKE: 20 MINUTES

FYI

The batter for these muffins can be stored in the refrigerator up to four weeks, so you can bake these hearty muffins whenever you want them.

1 (15-ounce) package wheat bran flakes cereal with raisins
5 cups all-purpose flour
3 cups sugar
1 tablespoon plus 2 teaspoons baking soda
1 teaspoon salt

4 large eggs, lightly beaten
1 quart buttermilk
1 cup shortening, melted

1 Combine first 5 ingredients in a large bowl; make a well in center of mixture.

2 Combine eggs, buttermilk, and shortening; add to dry ingredients, stirring just until dry ingredients are moistened. Cover and chill at least 8 hours and up to 4 weeks.

3 To bake, spoon batter into greased muffin pans, filling two-thirds full. Bake at 350° for 20 to 25 minutes or until golden. Remove from pans immediately. Yield: 5½ dozen.

Spoon Rolls

PREP: 14 MINUTES; CHILL: 8 HOURS; BAKE: 30 MINUTES

1 package active dry yeast
2 cups warm water (105° to 115°), divided

½ cup butter or margarine, melted
4 cups self-rising flour
¼ cup sugar
1 large egg, lightly beaten

1 Combine yeast and ¼ cup warm water in a 1-cup liquid measuring cup; let stand 5 minutes.

2 Combine yeast mixture, remaining 1¾ cups warm water, butter, and remaining ingredients in a large bowl, stirring until smooth. Cover and chill batter at least 8 hours and up to 3 days.

3 Stir batter; spoon into greased muffin pans, filling two-thirds full. Bake at 350° for 30 minutes or until lightly browned. Remove from pans immediately. Yield: about 1½ dozen.

Overnight Coffee Cake

Overnight Coffee Cake

PREP: 15 MINUTES; CHILL: 8 HOURS; BAKE: 30 MINUTES

2 cups all-purpose flour
1 teaspoon baking soda
1 teaspoon baking powder
½ teaspoon salt
¾ cup sugar
½ cup firmly packed brown sugar
1 teaspoon ground cinnamon
⅔ cup butter or margarine,
     melted
1 cup buttermilk
2 large eggs

½ cup firmly packed brown sugar
½ cup chopped pecans
1 teaspoon ground cinnamon

1 Combine first 10 ingredients in a large mixing bowl. Beat at low speed of an electric mixer until moistened; beat at medium speed 3 minutes. Spoon batter into a greased and floured 13- x 9- x 2-inch pan. Cover and chill 8 to 12 hours.

2 Combine ½ cup brown sugar, pecans, and 1 teaspoon cinnamon; place in an airtight container until ready to bake coffee cake.

3 Sprinkle batter with brown sugar mixture. Bake at 350° for 30 to 35 minutes or until a wooden pick inserted in center comes out clean. Serve warm. Yield: 15 servings.

FYI

To bake Overnight Coffee Cake immediately after preparing it, bake at 350° for 25 minutes or until a wooden pick inserted in the center comes out clean.

Wine-Marinated Fruit

PREP: 12 MINUTES; MARINATE: 2 HOURS

Ascorbic-citric powder
2 medium-size ripe pears,
   unpeeled and sliced
2 Red Delicious apples, unpeeled
   and sliced
2 bananas, sliced
2 peaches, peeled and sliced
1 pint fresh strawberries, sliced

2 tablespoons sugar
1½ cups Sauterne or other sweet
   white wine

2 tablespoons flaked coconut,
   toasted
Garnish: whole fresh strawberries

1 To prevent fruits from darkening, use commercial ascorbic-citric powder according to manufacturer's directions. Toss fruits separately in prepared solution; drain.

2 Layer fruits in a 13- x 9- x 2-inch baking dish, sprinkling each layer lightly with sugar. Pour wine over fruit mixture. Cover and marinate in refrigerator at least 2 hours.

3 Transfer fruit mixture to a serving bowl; sprinkle with toasted coconut. Garnish, if desired. Serve fruit mixture immediately with a slotted spoon. Yield: 10 servings.

Wine-Marinated Fruit

Caramel Toffee Bombe

PREP: 15 MINUTES; FREEZE: 8 HOURS

1⅓ cups gingersnap cookie crumbs (about 20 cookies)

¼ cup butter or margarine, melted

1 quart vanilla ice cream, softened

4 (1.4-ounce) English toffee-flavored candy bars, crushed

1 (12-ounce) jar caramel topping

½ cup chopped pecans, toasted

1 Line a 2-quart bowl with heavy-duty plastic wrap. Combine cookie crumbs and butter; press into prepared bowl. Combine ice cream and crushed candy; spoon into bowl. Cover and freeze at least 8 hours.

2 Combine caramel topping and chopped pecans; set aside.

3 To serve, let bombe stand at room temperature 5 minutes. Invert onto a serving plate; remove bowl and plastic wrap. Cut bombe into wedges; serve immediately with caramel topping mixture. Yield: 8 servings.

Reach for your food processor to crumble cookies and crush candy quickly.

Cookies and Cream Crunch

PREP: 20 MINUTES; FREEZE: 8 HOURS

1 (20-ounce) package cream-filled chocolate sandwich cookies, crushed

1 cup chopped pecans

½ cup butter, melted

½ gallon vanilla ice cream, softened

1 Combine first 3 ingredients; press half of mixture firmly in bottom of a lightly buttered 13- x 9- x 2-inch pan. Freeze 5 minutes.

2 Spread ice cream over crumb mixture in pan. Sprinkle remaining half of crumb mixture over ice cream; gently pressing crumb mixture into ice cream. Cover and freeze at least 8 hours.

3 To serve, let stand at room temperature 5 minutes; cut into squares. Yield: 15 servings.

The best way to trim time and trouble when you cook is to plan ahead. And you can depend on these make-ahead mixes and sauces to be your building blocks for quick and easy meals. Start with these five basic recipes,

JUMP-START COOKING

and you'll be able to whip out 12 family favorites. Stir **QUICK BAKING MIX** into biscuits, muffins, and waffles. Or use **GROUND CHUCK MIX** as a base for chili, spaghetti, and stuffed peppers. You can do it all in a matter of minutes when you have these basics on hand.

Grilled Chicken-Pasta Salad (page 225)

Marinara Sauce

USED FOR

Baked Ziti and Grilled Chicken-Pasta Salad

—⊰⊱—

Marinara Sauce

PREP: 6 MINUTES; COOK: 24 MINUTES

FYI

If you don't have a garlic press, create your own. Place a garlic clove between two pieces of heavy-duty plastic wrap, and crush the garlic with a meat mallet or the flat side of a chef's knife.

1 cup chopped onion
4 cloves garlic, pressed
2 tablespoons olive oil

4 (28-ounce) cans whole
    tomatoes, drained and
    chopped
¼ cup lemon juice
2 tablespoons dried Italian
    seasoning
4 bay leaves

1 Cook onion and garlic in hot oil in a Dutch oven over medium-high heat, stirring constantly, until tender.

2 Stir in tomato and remaining 3 ingredients; bring to a boil. Reduce heat; simmer 20 minutes, stirring occasionally. Discard bay leaves; cool. Refrigerate up to 1 week. Yield: 8 cups.

Baked Ziti

PREP: 9 MINUTES; COOK: 23 MINUTES

FYI

Add a tablespoon of vegetable oil to the cooking water to keep the pasta from sticking together and the water from foaming up and over the sides of the pan.

1 pound mild Italian sausage,
    casings removed
½ pound ground chuck
1 small onion, chopped
12 ounces ziti, cooked according
    to package directions
4 cups Marinara Sauce (above)

1 pound sliced mozzarella cheese,
    divided
¼ cup grated Parmesan cheese

1 Cook first 3 ingredients in a Dutch oven until meat is browned, stirring until it crumbles. Drain. Stir in pasta and Marinara Sauce.

2 Spoon half of meat mixture into a greased 13- x 9- x 2-inch baking dish; top with half of mozzarella and remaining meat mixture. Bake, uncovered, at 375° for 10 minutes or until heated. Top with remaining mozzarella and Parmesan; bake 5 minutes or until cheeses melt. Yield: 8 servings.

Grilled Chicken-Pasta Salad

PREP: 8 MINUTES; MARINATE: 8 HOURS; COOK: 20 MINUTES

4 ounces bow-tie pasta, uncooked
½ cup commercial Italian salad dressing, divided

2 skinned and boned chicken breast halves

½ small cucumber
1 cup Marinara Sauce (facing page)

1 Cook pasta according to package directions; drain. Rinse pasta with cold water; drain well. Place pasta in a large heavy-duty, zip-top plastic bag. Pour 2 tablespoons dressing over pasta. Seal bag; shake gently to coat pasta. Marinate in refrigerator 8 hours, shaking bag occasionally.

2 Place chicken in a large heavy-duty, zip-top plastic bag. Pour remaining ¼ cup plus 2 tablespoons dressing over chicken. Seal bag, and shake gently to coat chicken. Marinate in refrigerator 8 hours, turning bag occasionally.

3 Peel cucumber, if desired. Chop cucumber. Stir half of cucumber into Marinara Sauce. Reserve remaining cucumber.

4 Remove chicken from marinade, discarding marinade. Grill chicken, covered, over medium-hot coals (350° to 400°) 5 minutes on each side or until done.

5 Arrange pasta on individual serving plates. Spoon Marinara Sauce over pasta; top with chicken breasts, and sprinkle with remaining chopped cucumber. Yield: 2 servings.

F/*I*

If you're watching your calories and fat, substitute reduced fat or nonfat salad dressing.

Stuffed Peppers (facing page)

Ground Chuck Mix

PREP: 18 MINUTES; COOK: 35 MINUTES

FYI

Use a food processor to chop or mince celery, garlic, onions, and green pepper quickly.

4 **pounds ground chuck**
8 **stalks celery, chopped**
4 **cloves garlic, minced**
3 **medium onions, chopped**
1 **large green pepper, seeded and chopped**

2 **(14-ounce) bottles ketchup**
1 **(15-ounce) can tomato sauce**
¼ **cup Worcestershire sauce**
1 **tablespoon salt**
1 **teaspoon pepper**

1 Cook first 5 ingredients in a Dutch oven over medium-high heat until meat is browned, stirring until it crumbles. Drain.

2 Stir ketchup and remaining ingredients into meat mixture; bring to a boil. Reduce heat, and simmer, uncovered, 20 minutes, stirring occasionally. Remove from heat, and let cool completely.

3 Spoon meat mixture into 2- or 3-cup airtight containers or heavy-duty, zip-top freezer bags. Label and freeze up to 3 months. Thaw in refrigerator. Yield: 12 cups.

Ground Chuck Mix

USED FOR

Easy Spaghetti

Chili con Carne

Stuffed Peppers

Easy Spaghetti

PREP: 2 MINUTES; COOK: 10 MINUTES

3 cups Ground Chuck Mix
  (facing page), thawed
¼ teaspoon dried oregano
¼ teaspoon dried basil
⅛ teaspoon garlic salt

Hot cooked spaghetti
Grated Parmesan cheese

1 Combine first 4 ingredients in a saucepan; bring to a boil. Reduce heat, and simmer, uncovered, 10 minutes, stirring occasionally.

2 Serve sauce over hot cooked spaghetti; sprinkle with Parmesan cheese. Yield: 3 servings.

For maximum flavor from dried herbs, rub them between the palms of your hands, or crush them with your fingertips.

Chili con Carne

PREP: 2 MINUTES; COOK: 10 MINUTES

2 cups Ground Chuck Mix
  (facing page), thawed
1 (16-ounce) can kidney beans,
  undrained
1 tablespoon chili powder
⅛ teaspoon hot sauce

1 Combine all ingredients in a large saucepan; bring to a boil. Reduce heat, and simmer, uncovered, 10 minutes, stirring occasionally. Yield: 3 cups.

Stuffed Peppers

PREP: 10 MINUTES; COOK: 33 MINUTES

2 medium-size green peppers
2 medium-size sweet red peppers

2 cups Ground Chuck Mix (facing
  page), thawed
2 cups cooked rice

½ cup (2 ounces) shredded
  Cheddar cheese
Garnish: celery leaves

1 Cut off tops of peppers. Remove seeds and membranes. Cook peppers in boiling water 5 minutes; drain upside-down on paper towels.

2 Combine Ground Chuck Mix and rice; spoon into peppers. Place peppers in a baking dish. Cover and bake at 375° for 25 minutes.

3 Sprinkle with cheese; bake, uncovered, 3 minutes or until cheese melts. Arrange peppers on a platter; garnish, if desired. Yield: 4 servings.

Quick-Mix Waffles (page 230)

Quick Baking Mix

USED FOR

Quick-Mix Biscuits

Banana-Nut Muffins

Quick-Mix Pancakes

Quick-Mix Waffles

Marbled Coffee Cake

Quick Baking Mix

PREP: 15 MINUTES

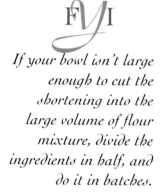

If your bowl isn't large enough to cut the shortening into the large volume of flour mixture, divide the ingredients in half, and do it in batches.

10 cups all-purpose flour
⅓ cup baking powder
1½ tablespoons salt
¼ cup sugar

2 cups shortening

1 Combine first 4 ingredients in a large bowl; stir with a wire whisk.

2 Cut shortening into dry ingredients with a pastry blender until mixture is crumbly. Store in an airtight container at room temperature up to 6 weeks. Yield: 13 cups.

Quick-Mix Biscuits

PREP: 5 MINUTES; BAKE: 10 MINUTES

2 cups Quick Baking Mix
    (facing page)
½ cup milk

1 Combine Quick Baking Mix and milk, stirring with a fork just until dry ingredients are moistened. Turn dough out onto a heavily floured surface; knead lightly 3 or 4 times.

2 Roll or pat dough to ½-inch thickness; cut with a floured 2-inch biscuit cutter. Place biscuits on an ungreased baking sheet; bake at 450° for 10 minutes or until lightly browned. Yield: 10 biscuits.

Banana-Nut Muffins

PREP: 10 MINUTES; BAKE: 20 MINUTES

1 (8-ounce) package cream cheese, softened
1 cup sugar
2 large eggs
1 cup mashed ripe banana
½ teaspoon vanilla extract
2 cups Quick Baking Mix
    (facing page)
½ cup chopped pecans

1 Beat cream cheese at high speed of an electric mixer until creamy; gradually add sugar, beating well. Add eggs; beat well. Add banana and vanilla; beat well. Stir in Quick Baking Mix and pecans.

2 Spoon batter into lightly greased muffin pans, filling two-thirds full. Bake at 375° for 20 to 22 minutes or until golden. Remove from pans immediately. Yield: 20 muffins.

FYI

Grease muffin pans with a light coating of vegetable cooking spray or a swipe of shortening. Or use paper baking cups to cut cleanup time.

Quick-Mix Pancakes

PREP: 5 MINUTES; COOK: 10 MINUTES

2 large eggs, lightly beaten
3 cups Quick Baking Mix
    (page 228)
1½ cups milk

1 Combine all ingredients; beat with a wire whisk until smooth.

2 For each pancake, pour about ¼ cup batter onto a hot, lightly greased griddle. Cook pancakes until tops are covered with bubbles and edges look cooked; turn and cook other side. Yield: 16 pancakes.

Quick-Mix Waffles

PREP: 10 MINUTES; BAKE: 15 MINUTES

FYI

While your waffle iron is out, why not make a double batch and freeze the left-overs? Just pop the frozen waffles into the toaster or toaster oven as you would commercial frozen waffles.

2 large eggs, separated
1⅓ cups milk
2 tablespoons vegetable oil
2 cups Quick Baking Mix
    (page 228)

Garnish: fresh raspberries

1 Beat egg yolks in a medium bowl; add milk and oil. Add Quick Baking Mix, stirring until smooth.

2 Beat egg whites at high speed of an electric mixer until stiff peaks form; gently fold beaten whites into batter.

3 Spoon 1 cup batter onto a pre-heated, oiled waffle iron; spread batter to edges. Bake until lightly browned. Repeat procedure with remaining batter. Garnish, if desired. Yield: 12 (4-inch) waffles.

Marbled Coffee Cake

PREP: 18 MINUTES; BAKE: 25 MINUTES

2 cups Quick Baking Mix
    (page 228)
¼ cup sugar
¾ cup milk
1 large egg

2 tablespoons molasses
½ teaspoon ground cinnamon
½ teaspoon ground nutmeg

¼ cup firmly packed brown sugar
2 tablespoons Quick Baking Mix
¼ teaspoon ground cinnamon
1 tablespoon butter or margarine

1 Combine first 4 ingredients in a mixing bowl; beat at medium speed of an electric mixer until smooth.

2 Reserve 1 cup batter. Stir molasses, ½ teaspoon cinnamon, and nutmeg into remaining batter.

3 Place spoonfuls of reserved 1 cup plain batter into a greased 8-inch square pan in a checkerboard pattern. Spoon spiced batter in spaces around plain batter; swirl batters together with a knife to create a marbled effect.

4 Combine brown sugar, 2 tablespoons Quick Baking Mix, and ¼ teaspoon cinnamon. Cut in butter with a pastry blender until mixture is crumbly. Sprinkle mixture over swirled batter. Bake at 375° for 25 minutes or until a wooden pick inserted in center comes out clean. Serve warm. Yield: 9 servings.

USED FOR

Quick-and-Easy Brownies

Quick-and-Easy Brownies

Brownie Mix

PREP: 10 MINUTES

*F*Y*I*

If your bowl is too small to hold this volume of mix, halve the ingredients, and mix it in batches.

4 cups all-purpose flour
1 tablespoon plus 1 teaspoon
    baking powder
1 tablespoon salt
5 cups sugar
2 cups cocoa

2 cups shortening

1 Combine first 5 ingredients in a large bowl; stir with a wire whisk.

2 Cut in shortening with a pastry blender until mixture is crumbly. Store in an airtight container at room temperature up to 6 weeks. Yield: 12 cups.

Quick-and-Easy Brownies

PREP: 5 MINUTES; BAKE: 35 MINUTES

3 large eggs, lightly beaten
3 cups Brownie Mix (above)
½ cup chopped pecans
1½ teaspoons vanilla extract

1 Combine all ingredients; spoon into a greased 8-inch square pan. Bake at 350° for 35 minutes. Cool. Cut into squares. Yield: 16 brownies.

Perfect Pastry Mix

USED FOR

Single-Crust Pastry Shell

—⁘—

Perfect Pastry Mix

PREP: 10 MINUTES

7 cups all-purpose flour
1 tablespoon salt

2 cups shortening

1 Combine flour and salt in a large bowl; stir with a wire whisk.

2 Cut shortening into dry ingredients with a pastry blender until mixture is crumbly. Store in an airtight container at room temperature up to 6 weeks. Yield: 8¾ cups.

Single-Crust Pastry Shell

PREP: 10 MINUTES; BAKE: 12 MINUTES

3 to 4 tablespoons cold water
1¼ cups Perfect Pastry Mix
    (above)

1 Sprinkle cold water (1 tablespoon at a time) evenly over Perfect Pastry Mix; stir with a fork just until dry ingredients are moistened. Shape dough into a ball.

2 Roll ball of dough to ⅛-inch thickness on a lightly floured surface. Place in a 9-inch pieplate; trim off excess pastry around edges. Fold edges under, and flute or crimp.

3 For baked pastry shell, prick bottom and sides of pastry shell with a fork. Bake at 425° for 12 to 15 minutes or until golden. Yield: one 9-inch pastry shell.

FYI

For a double crust, double these ingredients. Roll out half of dough, and place in pieplate; add filling. Roll rest of dough one inch larger than top of pieplate; place over filling. Fold overhang under, pressing to seal. Flute edges, and cut slits in top crust. Bake as recipe directs.

INDEX

234

CREDITS

OXMOOR HOUSE WISHES TO THANK THE FOLLOWING MERCHANTS:

Annieglass, Santa Cruz, CA
Augusta Glass Studio, Augusta, MO
Carolyn Rice Art Pottery, Marietta, GA
Charlotte & Co., Birmingham, AL
Christine's, Birmingham, AL
Churchill Weavers, Berea, KY
Cyclamen Studio, Berkeley, CA
The Holly Tree, Birmingham, AL
Kosta Boda, Kosta, Sweden
Lace in Stone, Santa Cruz, CA
Laufen Ceramic Tile, Tulsa, OK
Le Creuset of America, Inc., Yemassee, SC
Longaberger Baskets, Dresden, OH
The Loom Company, Aletha Soulé, New York, NY
MacKenzie-Childs, Ltd., Aurora, NY
Mama Ro, Portland, OR
Mesa International, Elkins, NH
Rezware, New York, NY
Rina Peleg Ceramics, Brooklyn, NY
Sabre Flatware, Dallas, TX
Swid Powell, New York, NY
Taitu, Dallas, TX
Timothy Weber Pottery, Northport, AL

ADDITIONAL PHOTOGRAPHY:
Ralph Anderson: pages 204, 214, 219, 220
Tina Evans: pages 206, 209

ADDITIONAL PHOTO STYLING:
Melanie J. Clarke: page 72
Virginia Cravens: pages 204, 206, 209, 214, 219, 220

METRIC EQUIVALENTS

The recipes that appear in this cookbook use the standard United States method for measuring liquid and dry or solid ingredients (teaspoons, tablespoons, and cups). The information in the following charts is provided to help cooks outside the U.S. successfully use these recipes. All equivalents are approximate.

Metric Equivalents for Different Types of Ingredients

A standard cup measure of a dry or solid ingredient will vary in weight depending on the type of ingredient. A standard cup of liquid is the same volume for any type of liquid. Use the following chart when converting standard cup measures to grams (weight) or milliliters (volume).

Standard Cup	Fine Powder (ex. flour)	Grain (ex. rice)	Granular (ex. sugar)	Liquid Solids (ex. butter)	Liquid (ex. milk)
1	140 g	150 g	190 g	200 g	240 ml
¾	105 g	113 g	143 g	150 g	180 ml
⅔	93 g	100 g	125 g	133 g	160 ml
½	70 g	75 g	95 g	100 g	120 ml
⅓	47 g	50 g	63 g	67 g	80 ml
¼	35 g	38 g	48 g	50 g	60 ml
⅛	18 g	19 g	24 g	25 g	30 ml

Useful Equivalents for Liquid Ingredients by Volume

¼ tsp				=	1 ml
½ tsp				=	2 ml
1 tsp				=	5 ml
3 tsp	=	1 tbls	= ½ fl oz	=	15 ml
	2 tbls	= ⅛ cup	= 1 fl oz	=	30 ml
	4 tbls	= ¼ cup	= 2 fl oz	=	60 ml
	5⅓ tbls	= ⅓ cup	= 3 fl oz	=	80 ml
	8 tbls	= ½ cup	= 4 fl oz	=	120 ml
	10⅔ tbls	= ⅔ cup	= 5 fl oz	=	160 ml
	12 tbls	= ¾ cup	= 6 fl oz	=	180 ml
	16 tbls	= 1 cup	= 8 fl oz	=	240 ml
	1 pt	= 2 cups	= 16 fl oz	=	480 ml
	1 qt	= 4 cups	= 32 fl oz	=	960 ml
			33 fl oz	=	1000 ml = 1 l

Useful Equivalents for Dry Ingredients by Weight

(To convert ounces to grams, multiply the number of ounces by 30.)

1 oz	=	1/16 lb	=	30 g
4 oz	=	¼ lb	=	120 g
8 oz	=	½ lb	=	240 g
12 oz	=	¾ lb	=	360 g
16 oz	=	1 lb	=	480 g

Useful Equivalents for Length

(To convert inches to centimeters, multiply the number of inches by 2.5.)

1 in			=	2.5 cm		
6 in	= ½ ft		=	15 cm		
12 in	= 1 ft		=	30 cm		
36 in	= 3 ft	= 1 yd	=	90 cm		
40 in			=	100 cm	=	1 m

Useful Equivalents for Cooking/Oven Temperatures

	Fahrenheit	Celcius	Gas Mark
Freeze Water	32° F	0° C	
Room Temperature	68° F	20° C	
Boil Water	212° F	100° C	
Bake	325° F	160° C	3
	350° F	180° C	4
	375° F	190° C	5
	400° F	200° C	6
	425° F	220° C	7
	450° F	230° C	8
Broil			Grill